ENJOY!
Aislin

AISLIN 14
MONTREAL
THE GAZETTE

This collection is dedicated to my five grandkids –
Connor, Jack, Morgan, Sydney and Luc – with hopes that
they may help to create a better world than we have.

The Wrecking Ball

and other recent cartoons by Aislin

With an introduction by Chantal Hébert

Text and cartoons by Terry Mosher

.ll.

The Wrecking Ball
by AISLIN

Text and cartoons by Terry Mosher
With an introduction by Chantal Hébert

Layout, design and electronic imaging: Mary Hughson

Cover image: AISLIN

Printed and bound in Canada by Marquis Book Printing Inc.

Library and Archives Canada Cataloguing in Publication

Aislin [Cartoons. Selections]   The wrecking ball / by Aislin ; text and cartoons by Terry Mosher ; with an introduction by Chantal Hébert.

ISBN 978-1-927535-55-4 (pbk.)

    1. Canadian wit and humor, Pictorial. 2. Québec (Province)--Politics and government--2012- --Caricatures and cartoons. 3. Canada--Politics and government--2006- --Caricatures and cartoons. I. Hébert, Chantal, 1954- writer of introduction II. Title.

NC1449.A37A4 2014   741.5›971   C2014-903387-7

Linda Leith Publishing gratefully acknowledges the support of SODEC.

www.lindaleith.com

Linda Leith Publishing Inc., P.O. Box 322, Station Victoria, Westmount QC H3Z 2V8 Canada

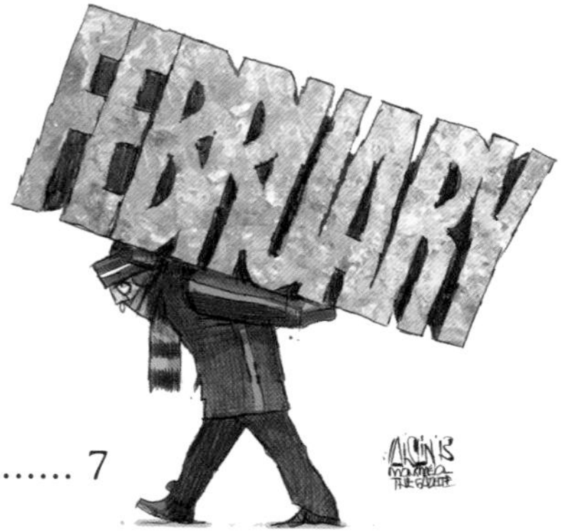
FEBRUARY

Table of Contents

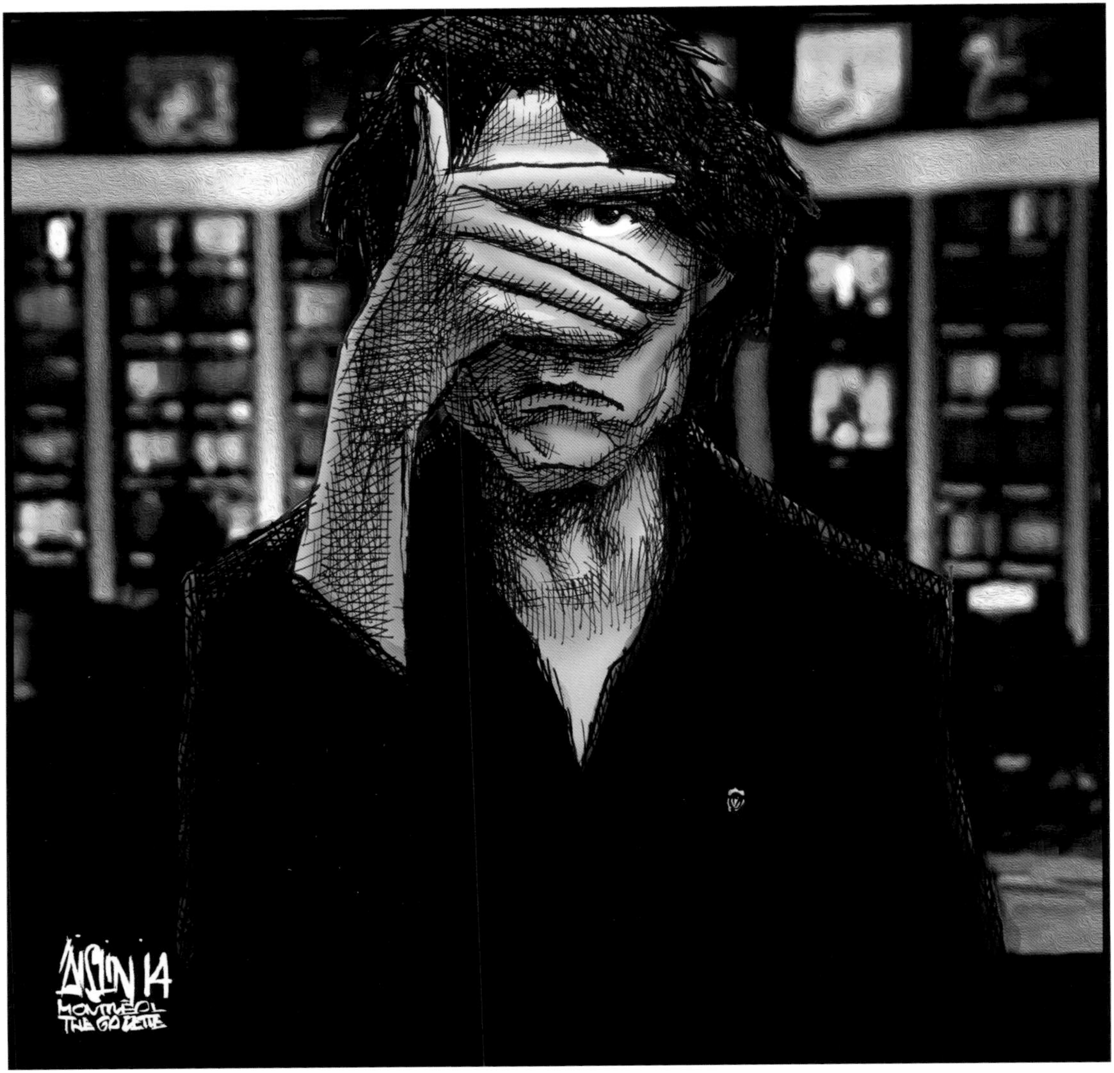
AISLIN 14
MONTREAL
THE GAZETTE

Introduction

It is a poorly kept secret that the dreams of editorial cartoonists are usually the stuff that our collective nightmares are made of. That has rarely been more true than over the past two years.

Think of the mayor of Toronto on crack cocaine; the handcuffs that have replaced the gold watch on the wrists of some of Quebec's veteran municipal politicians; the "walking dead" of the Canadian Senate coming back to haunt Prime Minister Stephen Harper; and the pictograms of to-be-banned religious symbols of the Parti Québécois.

Terry Mosher – or Aislin as he is known by scores of fans for his cutting-edge *Montreal Gazette* cartoons – has been at this for almost half a century. But even one as prescient as he is could not have fathomed the twists and turns of the recent past.

Rarely has political reality in Canada so consistently outdone fiction.

Who needs editorial cartoonists, you might ask, at a time when actual politicians are so keen on doing all the work for them?

Look to this collection for the answer. It will make you wonder whether to laugh or cry at the times we live in. It will also almost make it worthwhile to have endured the past two years.

– **Chantal Hébert**

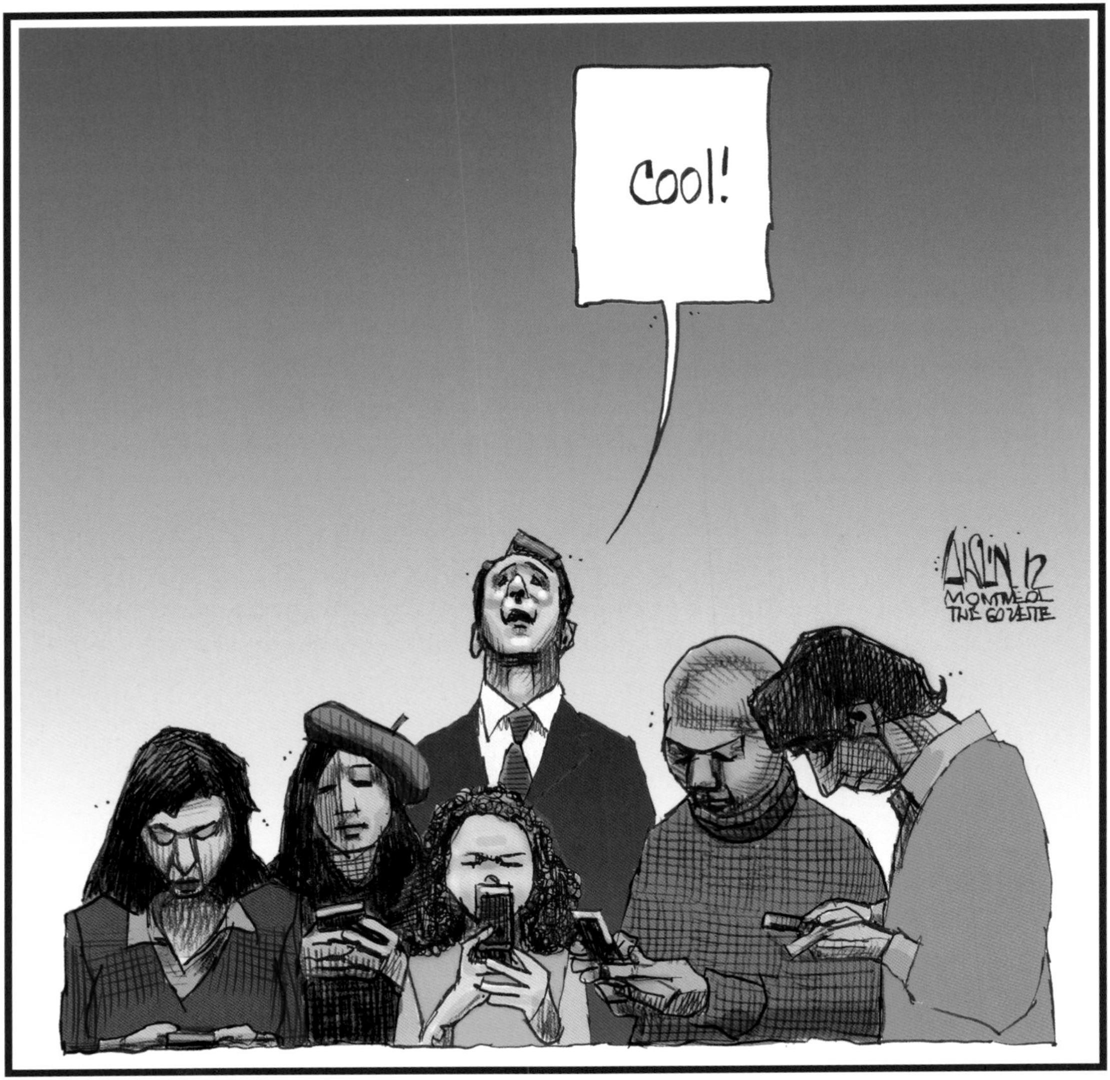
Cool!

Look up!

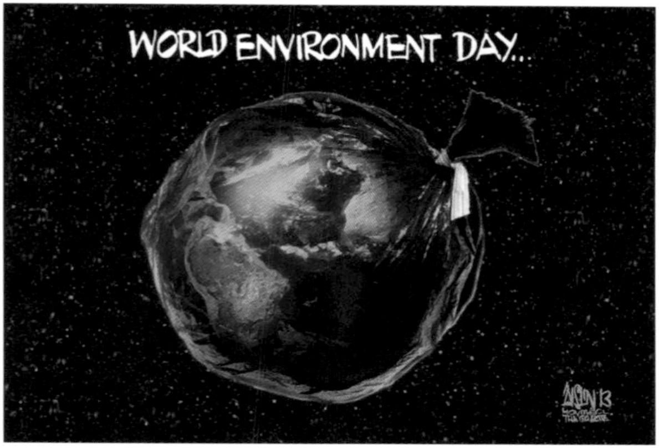
WORLD ENVIRONMENT DAY...

Welcome Aboard

In an increasingly complicated world, drawing cartoons remains a comparatively simple process – and a cheap one at that. There are no expensive film, video or photo shoots; no attendant assistants or staff; and – best of all – no meetings with anyone with the exception of yourself.

Then, with a two-dollar pencil and a sheet of paper (preferably acid-free), the cartoonist will start to sketch something on a subject that amuses, concerns, angers or even puzzles him or her.

Coming up with the idea is the thing, of course – an idea that your audience is going to understand, and that might just stand the test of time. I've drawn about twelve thousand cartoons during my long career, many of which I now consider eminently forgettable, but every so often there are real gems that you hope will be remembered.

Every few years, I go through five or six hundred of my most recent cartoons, boil them down to the ones I still like – and think that you might enjoy, too – and then publish another book.

So, welcome aboard! I hope you will enjoy this collection of Aislin cartoons from the last two very interesting years.

Tightrope walker asks for donations

ASSOCIATED PRESS

NIAGARA FALLS, N.Y. – Walking a high wire over Niagara Falls isn't only a dicey proposition, it turns out it's pretty pricey, too.

Daredevil Nik Wallenda [mates] his history-making, [...]-to-Canada walk by way of a [...] strung over the brink will [...] about $1.3 million. That in[...] fabrication and installation [...] custom-made steel wire, [...] and security on both sides [...] border, travel, and marketing[...]

A deal with ABC to tele[...] event live during prime t[...] day will offset some of h[...] es, the 33-year-old Wall[...] "But definitely not any[...]ere n[...] all of it."

There hasn't been much time to line up sponsors – the date of the walk was settled only about six

For $5[...] the wall[...] poster. [...] one pers[...] ccess t[...] [d]inn[...] no imme[...] Wallenda-taught backyard wire-w[alk]ing lesson, dinner and VIP [vie]wing, for $10,000.

"We need stuff like this," Wal-[...] says on the video. "We need things to encourage people that the impossible is actually possible."

Wallenda has agreed to pay Canadian authorities $105,000 for things like extra security, crowd control, fencing and portable toilets for the estimated 100,000 spectators. He also must supply a $50,000 letter [of] credit, which would [...] [...]ly in the event of a water [...]id Niagara Parks Comm[...]ir-person Janice Thomson.

ALL THESE CHEQUES ARE POST-DATED...

The world mourns the death of Nelson Mandela.

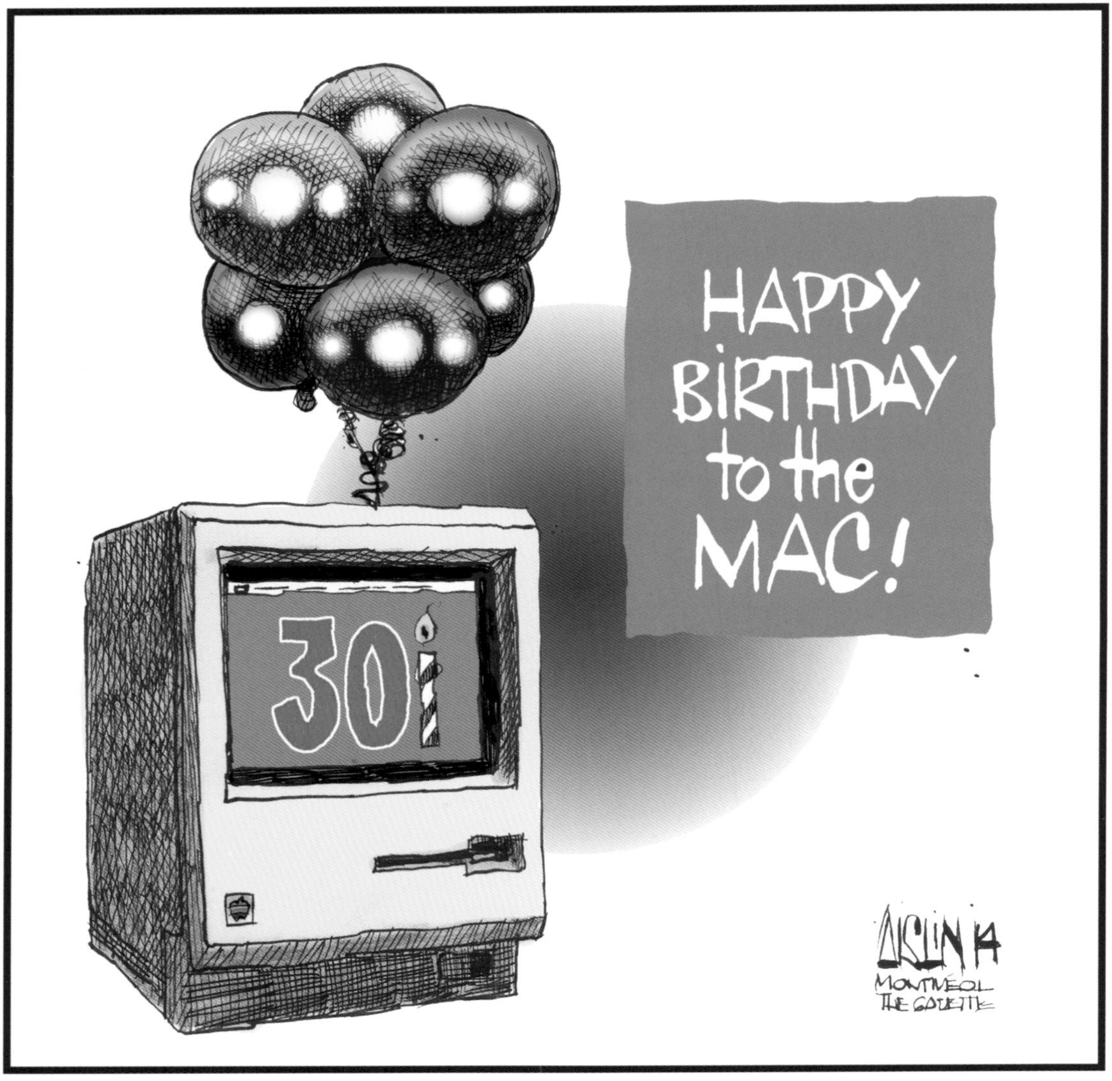
HAPPY BIRTHDAY to the MAC!
30
AISLIN '14
MONTREAL THE GAZETTE

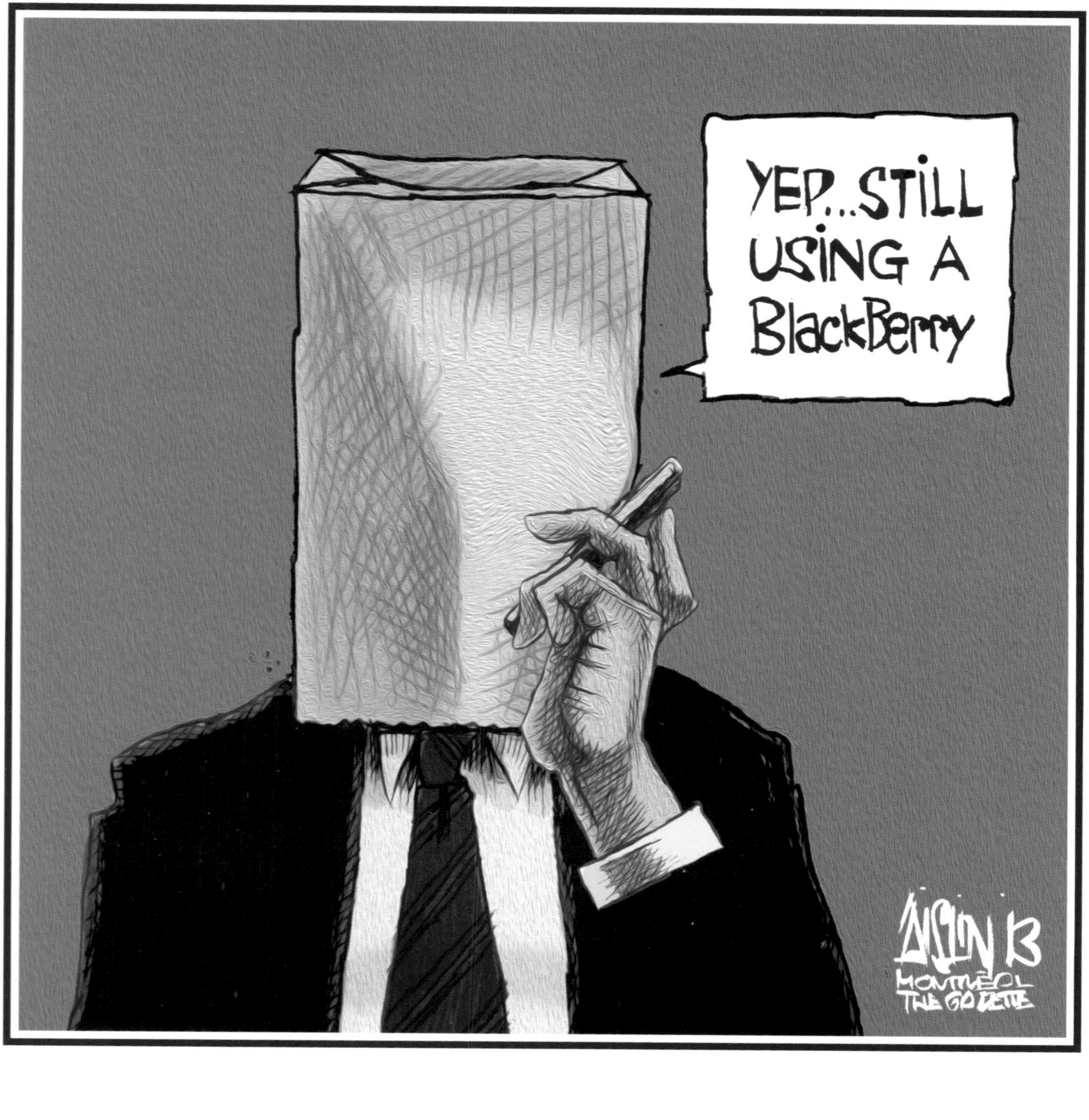
YEP...STILL USING A BlackBerry
AISLIN 13
MONTREAL THE GAZETTE

THEN: Blah...blah!

NOW: Blog...blog!

AISLIN 14
MONTREAL
THE GAZETTE

Apple and Google: Continuous smackdowns.

Drivers on cell phones are four times more likely to have accidents.

What! Ear buds at Montreal's Jazz Festival.

The average age of rock and roll concert-goers approaches sixty-five.

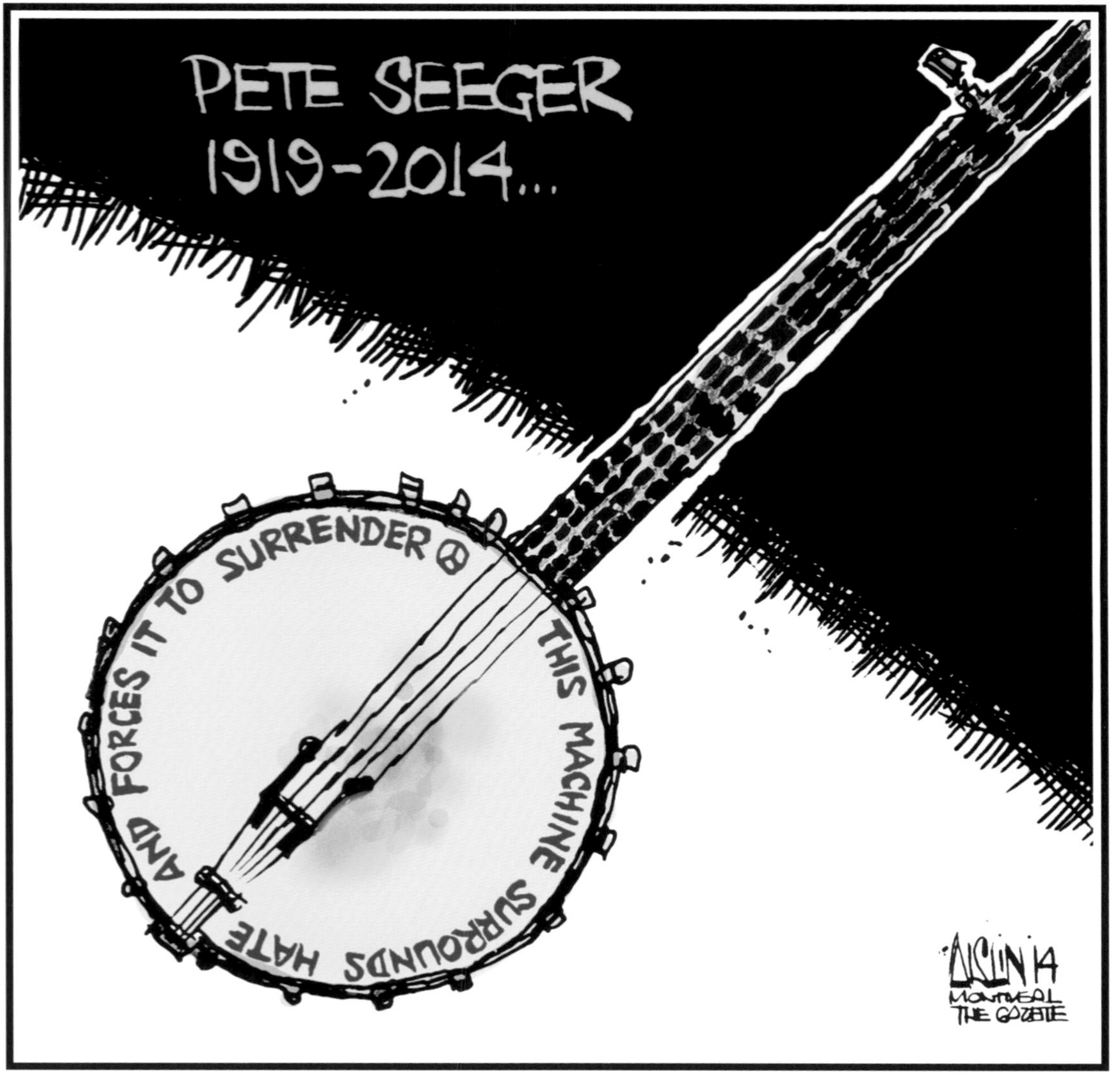

PETE SEEGER
1919-2014...
THIS MACHINE SURROUNDS HATE AND FORCES IT TO SURRENDER
AISLIN 14
MONTREAL THE GAZETTE

The winter of 2013-2014 is one of the most brutal in living memory.

Don't shoot the messenger!

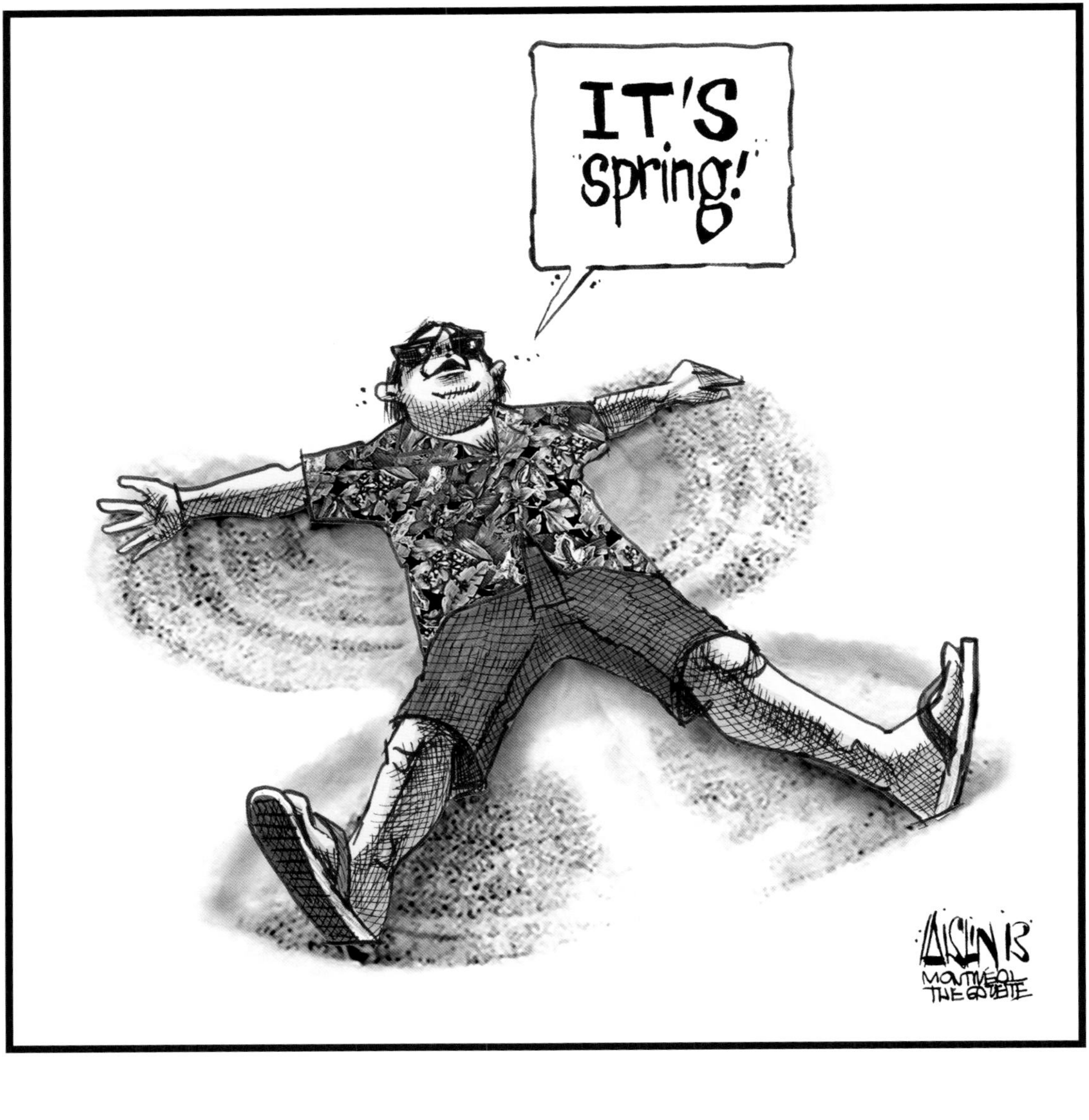
IT'S spring!
AISLIN 13
MONTRÉAL THE GAZETTE

The summer of 2012's extreme heat wave!

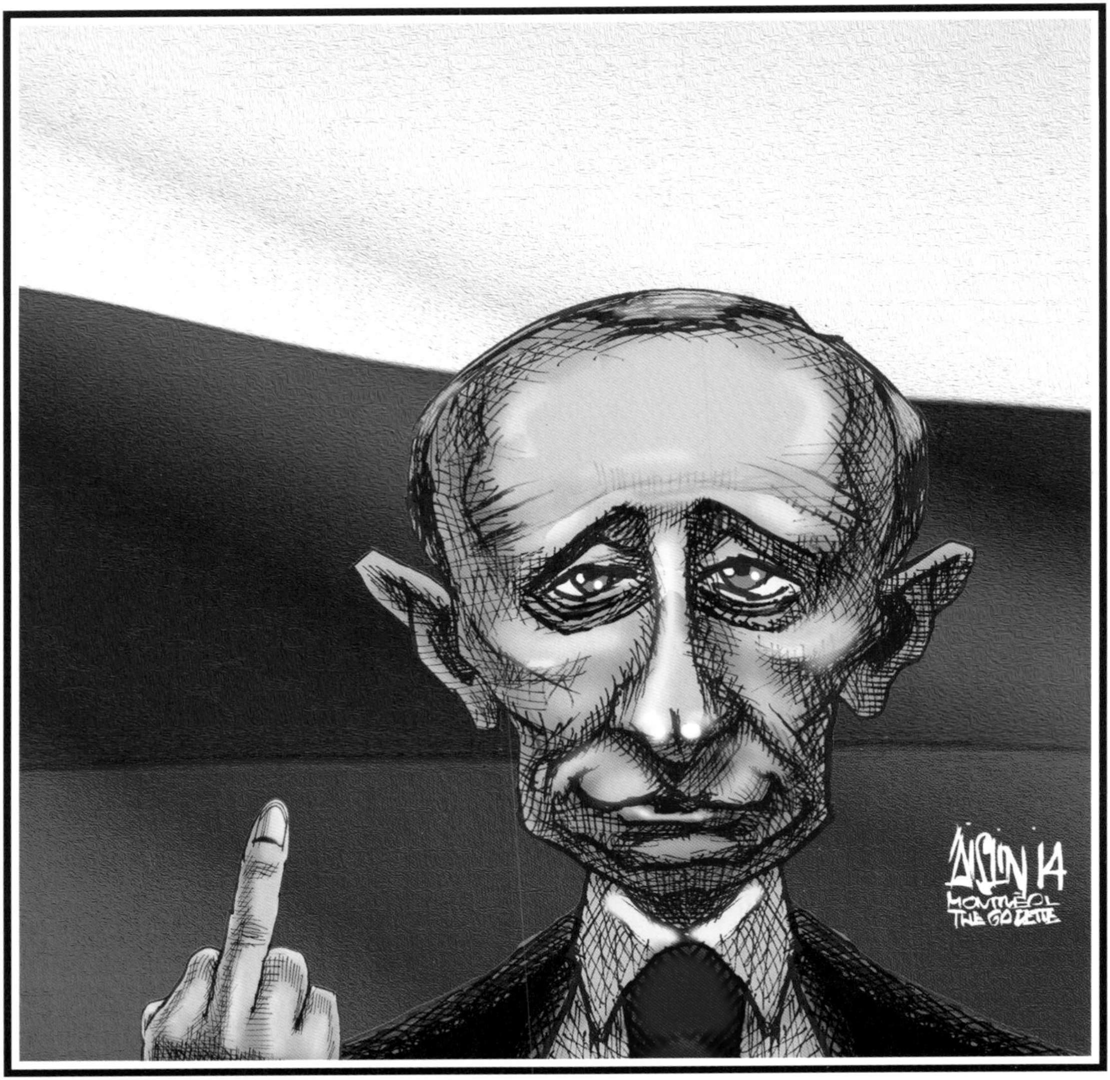
AISLIN 14
MONTREAL
THE GAZETTE

Vladimir Putin.

A suggestion on how to modernize the Roman Catholic Church.

Queen Elizabeth II celebrates her Diamond Jubilee...

...as do those closest to her.

The birth of Prince George.

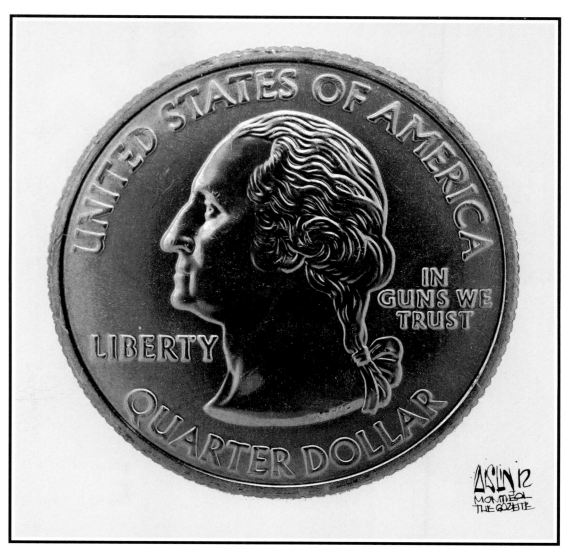

Spanish proverb: "When our friends are one-eyed, we try to see them in profile."

Universally recognized ominous symbols.

30

The elephant has long been the symbol of the Republican Party.

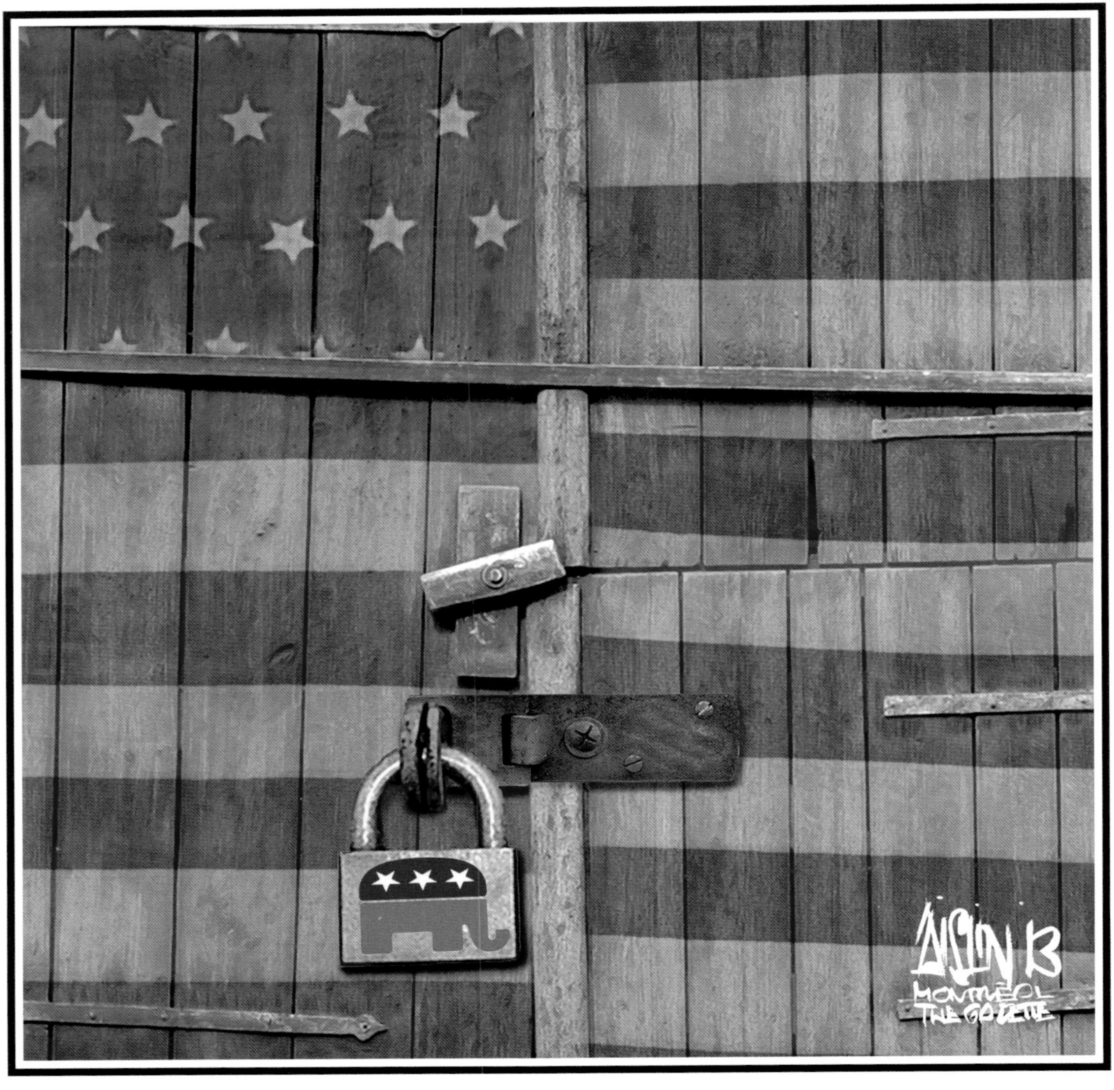
AISLIN 13
MONTREAL
THE GAZETTE

SEAL OF THE PRESIDENT OF THE DIVIDED STATES

E PLURIBUS UNUM

33

President Obama is hopeful of being re-elected in 2012...

QUESTION: SO WHAT DID MITT ROMNEY'S "BINDER FULL of WOMEN" LOOK LIKE?

...particularly when his Republican opponent, Mitt Romney, is always putting his foot in his mouth.

Whatever happened to "YES, WE CAN"?

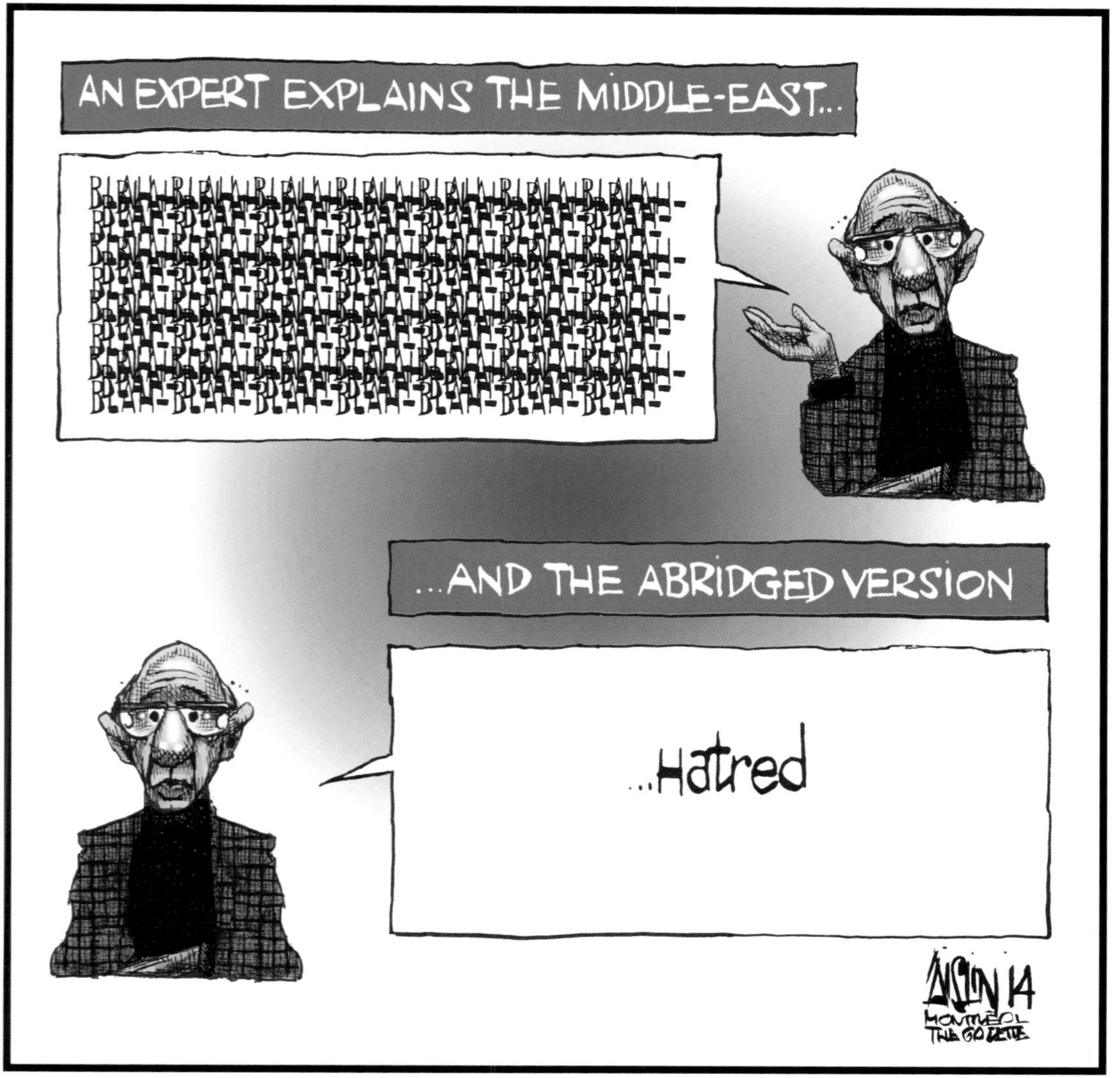
AN EXPERT EXPLAINS THE MIDDLE-EAST...
BLAH-BLAH-BLAH-BLAH-BLAH-BLAH-BLAH-
...AND THE ABRIDGED VERSION
...Hatred
AISLIN 14
MONTREAL THE GAZETTE

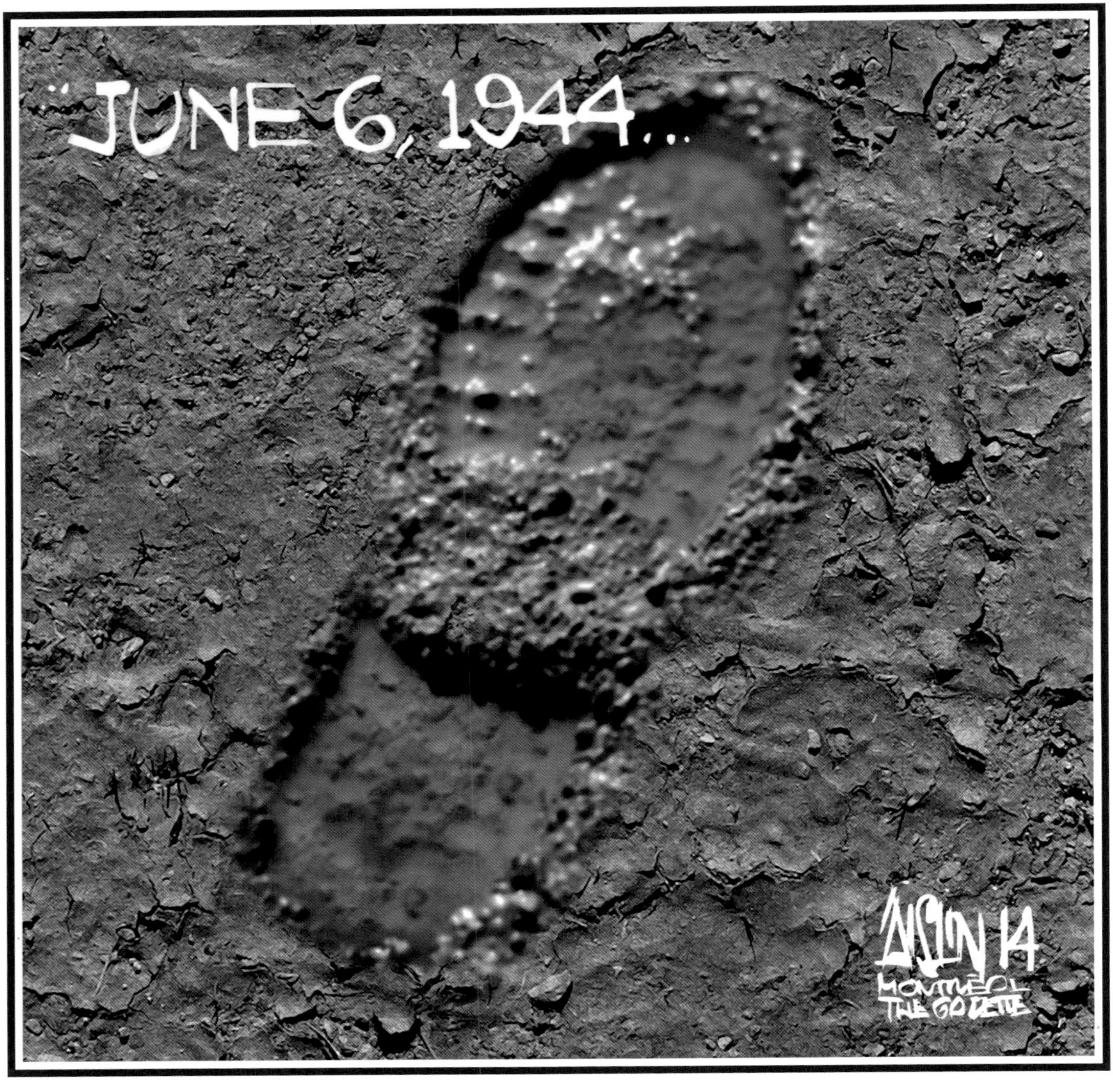
"JUNE 6, 1944...
AISLIN 14
MONTREAL
THE GAZETTE
70th anniversary of D-Day.

Canada

Stephen Harper is fond of saying that Canada is the best country in the world.

Well sure: Hockey, peacekeeping, bilingualism, multiculturalism, freedom, water, snow, Trans-Canada Highway, health care, the Rockies, winter sports, Tim Hortons, railways, decency, The Rocket, our great musicians, beer, Newfoundland, butter tarts, poutine, Tommy Douglas, curling, the Prairies, Alice Munro – all that.

But Canadians now produce more garbage than any nation on earth. We also watch more television, spend more time on the Internet and the telephone, and eat more donuts than anyone. Worst of all, Canada is one of the world's largest greenhouse gas emitters, thanks to the policies of Stephen Harper.

Is it any wonder that they were once called the Progressive Conservative Party of Canada, but that they dropped the word Progressive?

What happened? Why did the United States get Barack Obama – who would have made a perfect Canadian Prime Minister? And why did we get Stephen Harper – who would have made a great Republican American President?

Will the CBC eventually be carved up in the Conservative government's own image?

Radio-Canada tries (and fails) to rename itself by eliminating the word Canada.

Goodbye to the Canadian penny: 1858 – 2013.

MEMO #1: At Christmas, I gave a grandchild of mine a brand new $20 bill. She then sent me a note, profusely thanking me for the $60!...

MEMO #2: Some tips on how to separate those terrible new polymer bank notes...

New Canadian bank bills prove to be difficult to separate.

Oops! More of those embarrassing oil spills!

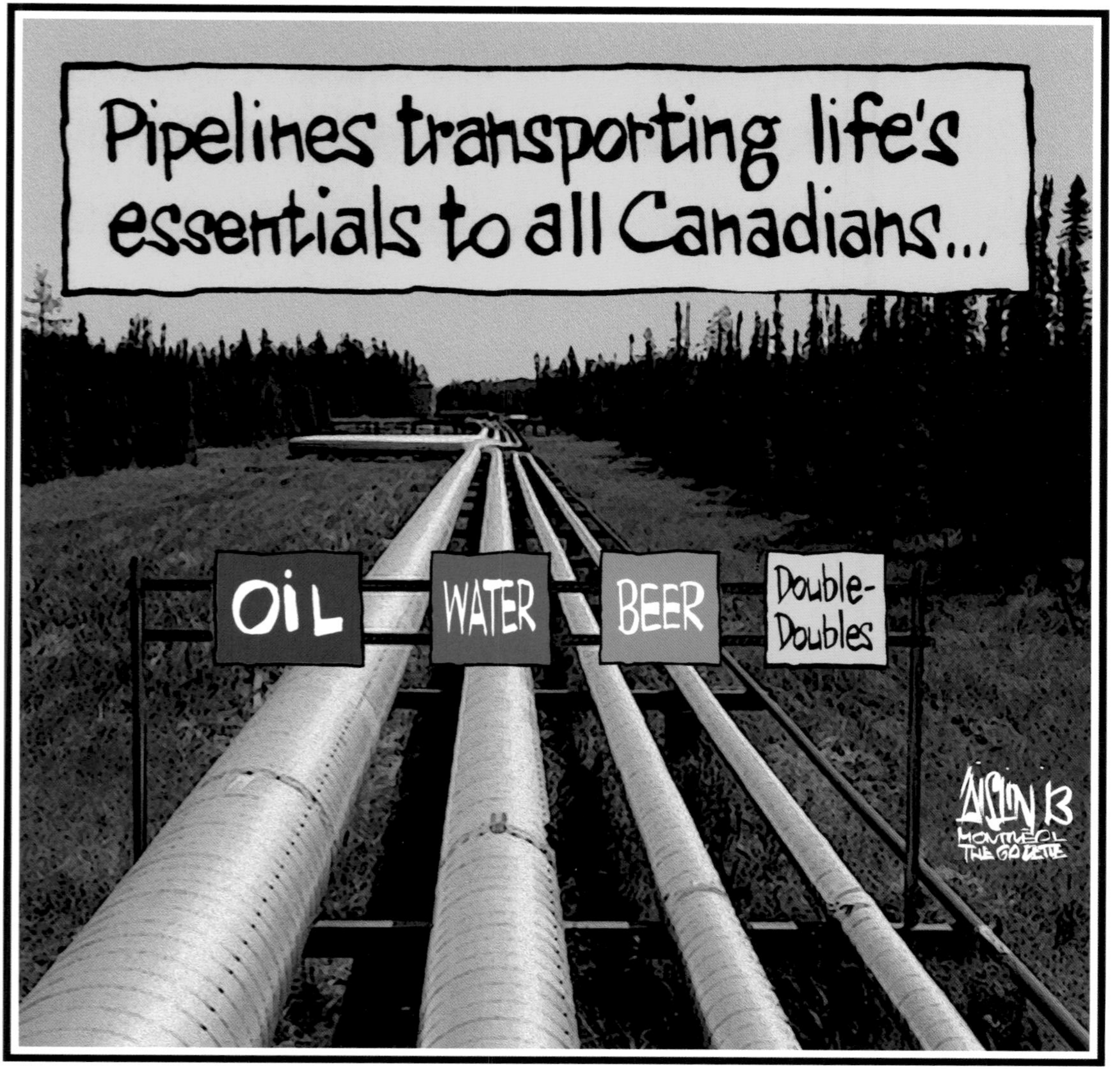
Pipelines transporting life's essentials to all Canadians...
OIL
WATER
BEER
Double-Doubles
AISLIN 13
MONTREAL THE GAZETTE

Canada is monitoring international communications.

Indigenous peoples' Idle No More movement gains momentum across Canada.

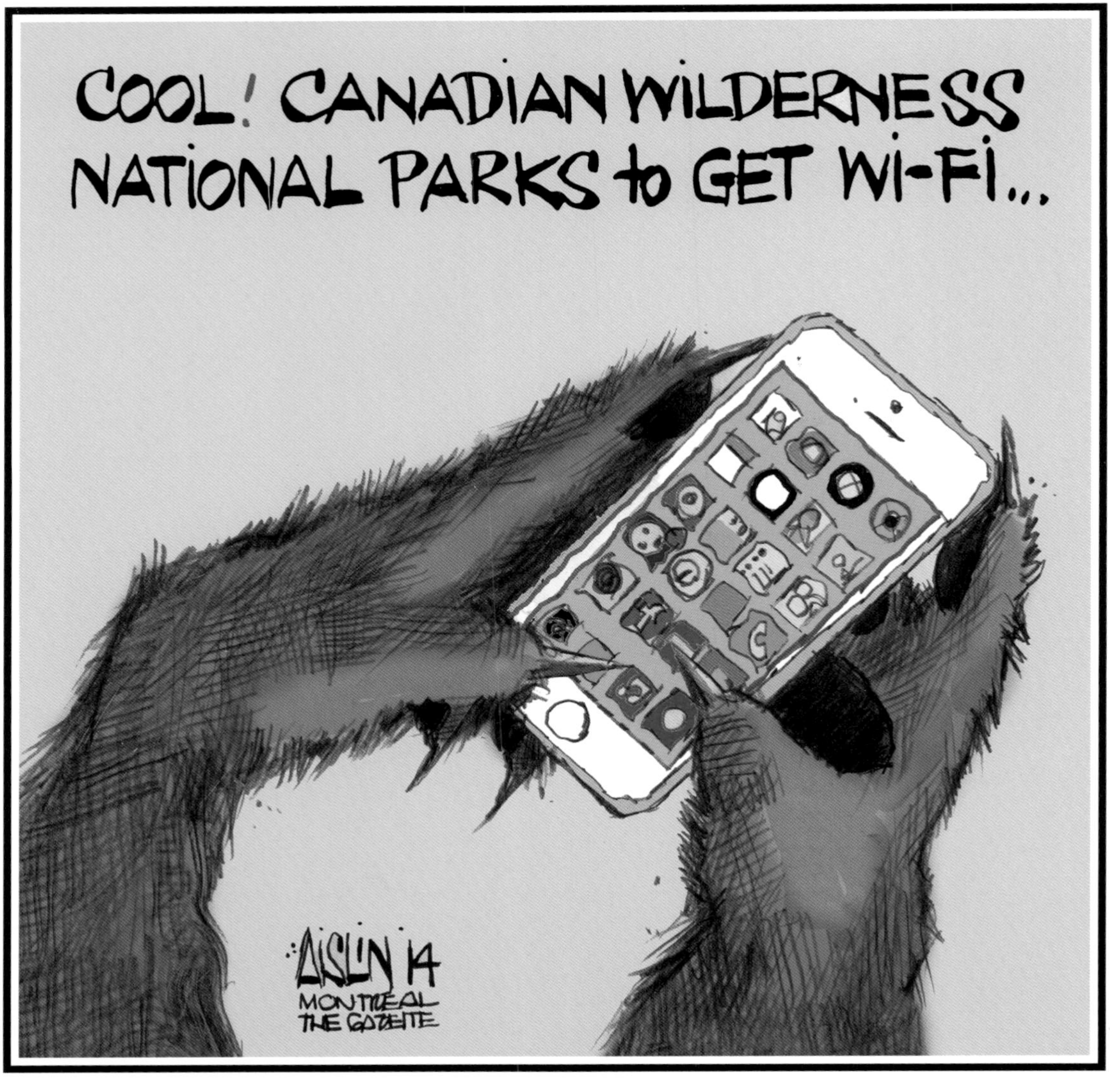
COOL! CANADIAN WILDERNESS NATIONAL PARKS to GET Wi-Fi...
AISLIN 14
MONTREAL
THE GAZETTE

200th anniversary of the War of 1812.

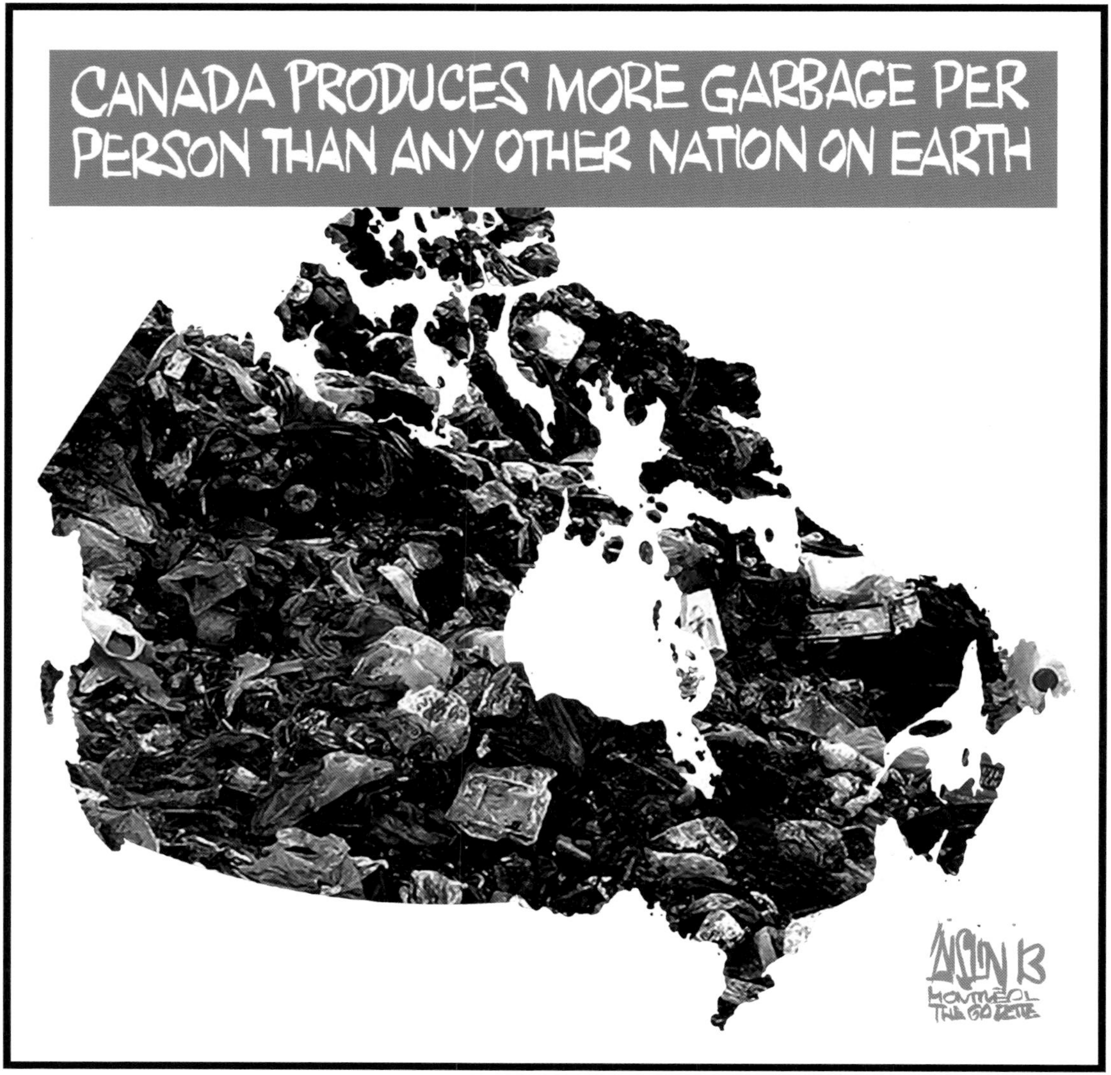
CANADA PRODUCES MORE GARBAGE PER PERSON THAN ANY OTHER NATION ON EARTH

Gang-related shootings are on the rise in Toronto.

The astonishing Toronto mayor, Rob Ford!

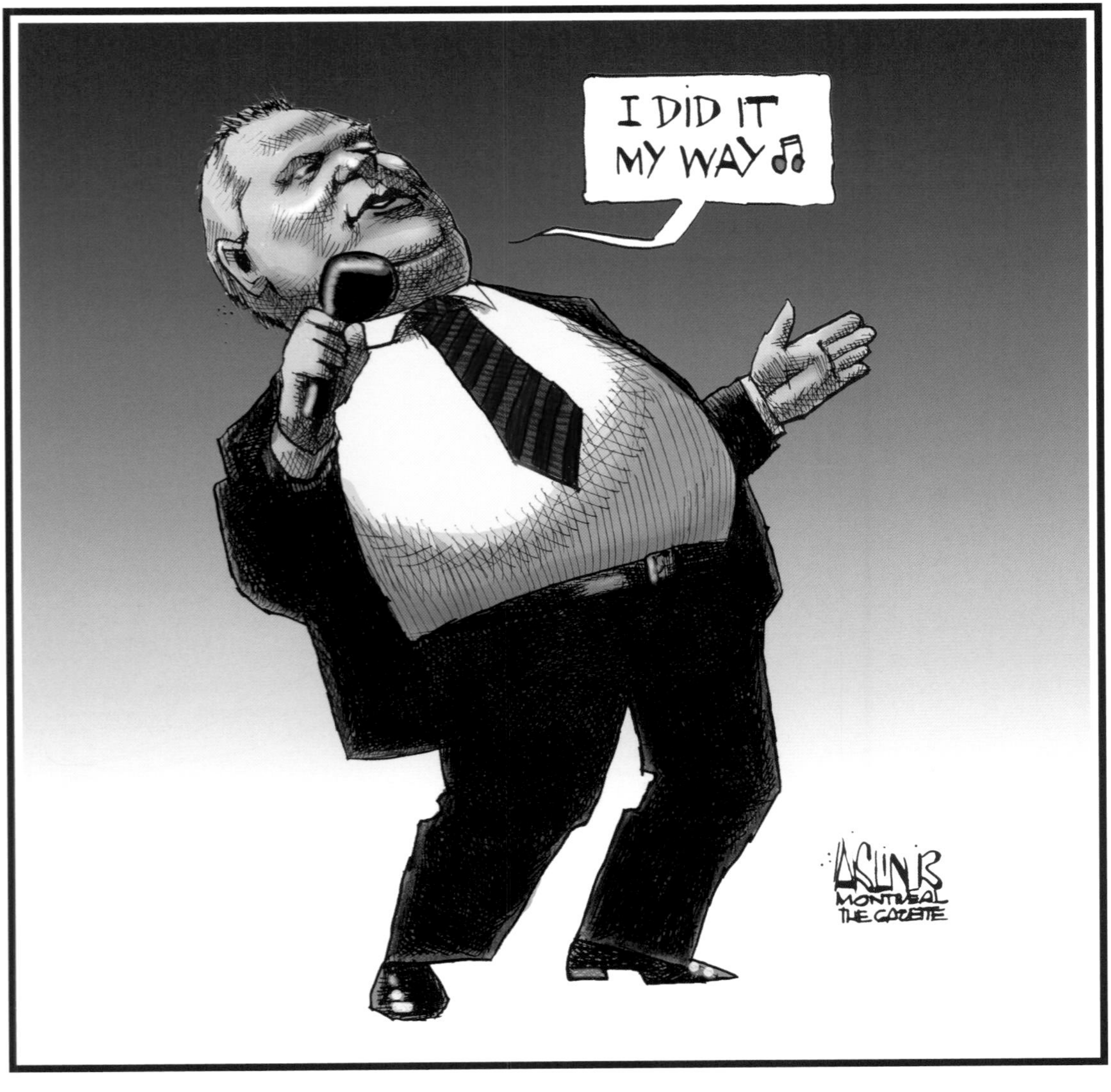
I DID IT MY WAY
AISLIN
MONTREAL
THE GAZETTE

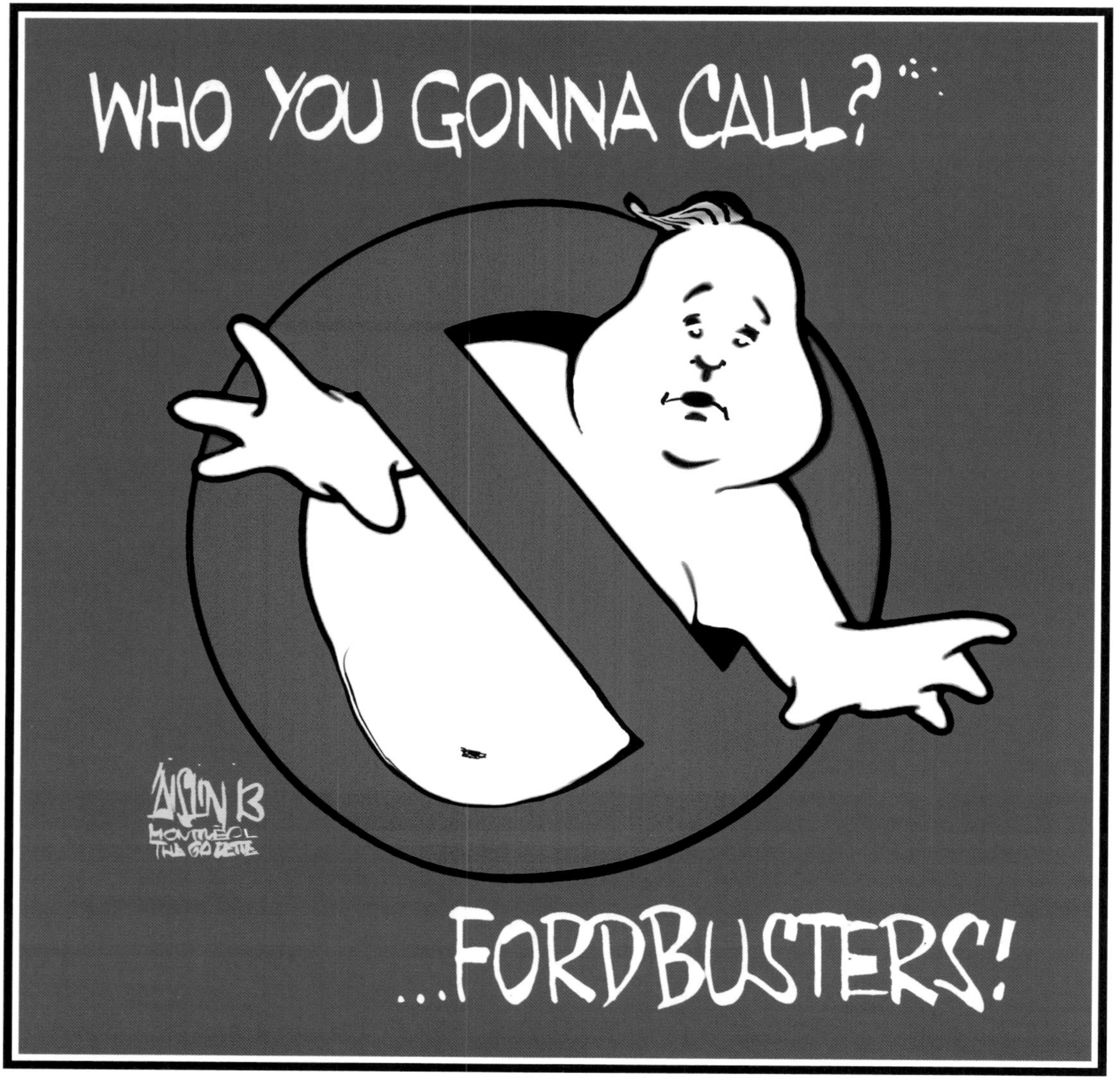
WHO YOU GONNA CALL?
...FORDBUSTERS!

When Justin Trudeau arrives in Ottawa, will it be in his father's old Mercedes?

Justin Trudeau is constantly accused of being a lightweight.

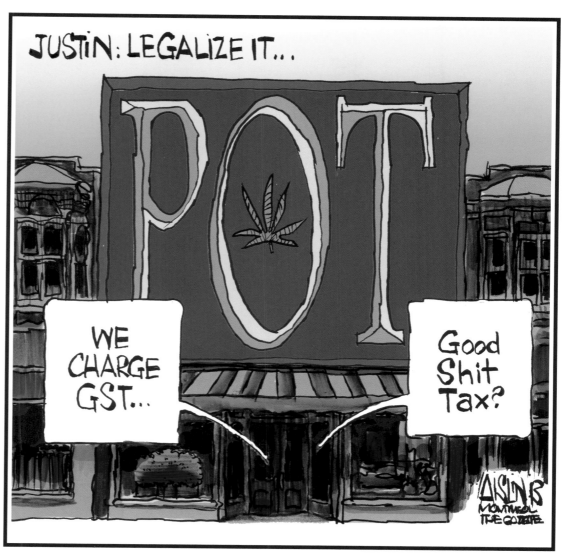

J.T. comes out for the legalization of marijuana.

THIS SUMMER, YOU'LL KNOW THE ELECTION CAMPAIGN IS ON WHEN YOU SEE TOM MULCAIR RIDING a HORSE...

Campaigning for the 2015 federal election begins.

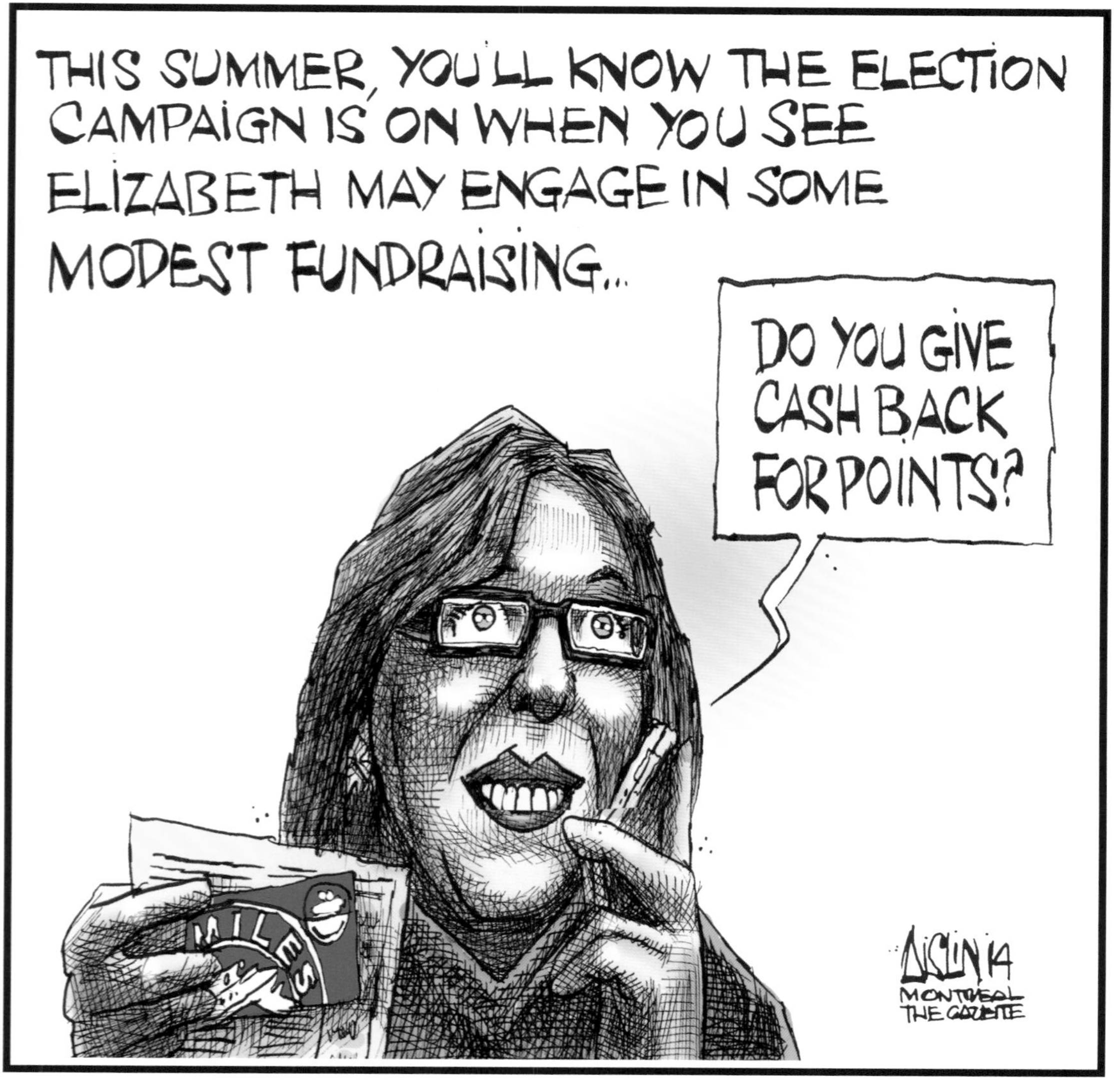
THIS SUMMER, YOU'LL KNOW THE ELECTION CAMPAIGN IS ON WHEN YOU SEE ELIZABETH MAY ENGAGE IN SOME MODEST FUNDRAISING...
DO YOU GIVE CASH BACK FOR POINTS?
MILES
AISLIN 14
MONTREAL THE GAZETTE

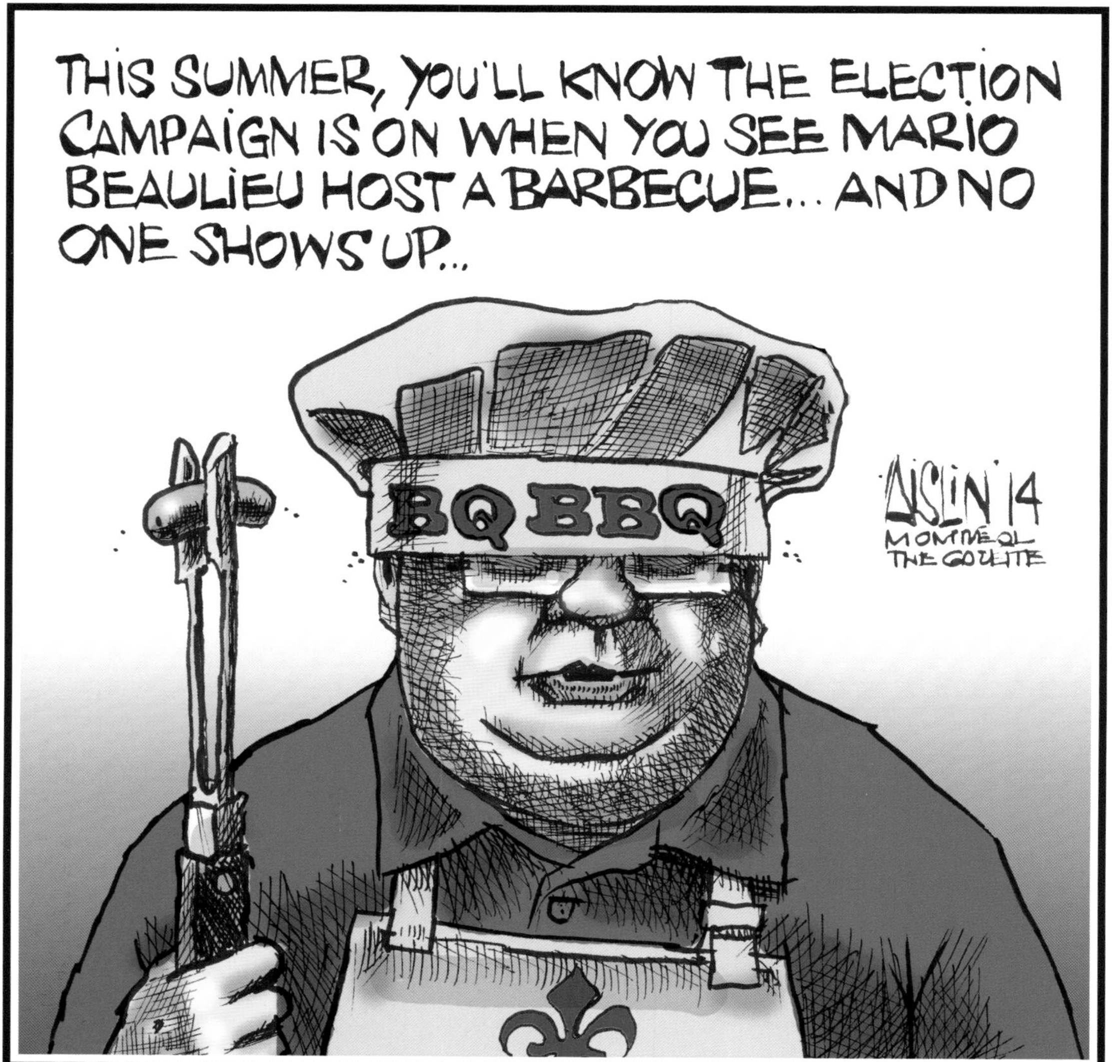
THIS SUMMER, YOU'LL KNOW THE ELECTION CAMPAIGN IS ON WHEN YOU SEE MARIO BEAULIEU HOST A BARBECUE... AND NO ONE SHOWS UP...
BQ BBQ
AISLIN '14
MONTREAL
THE GAZETTE

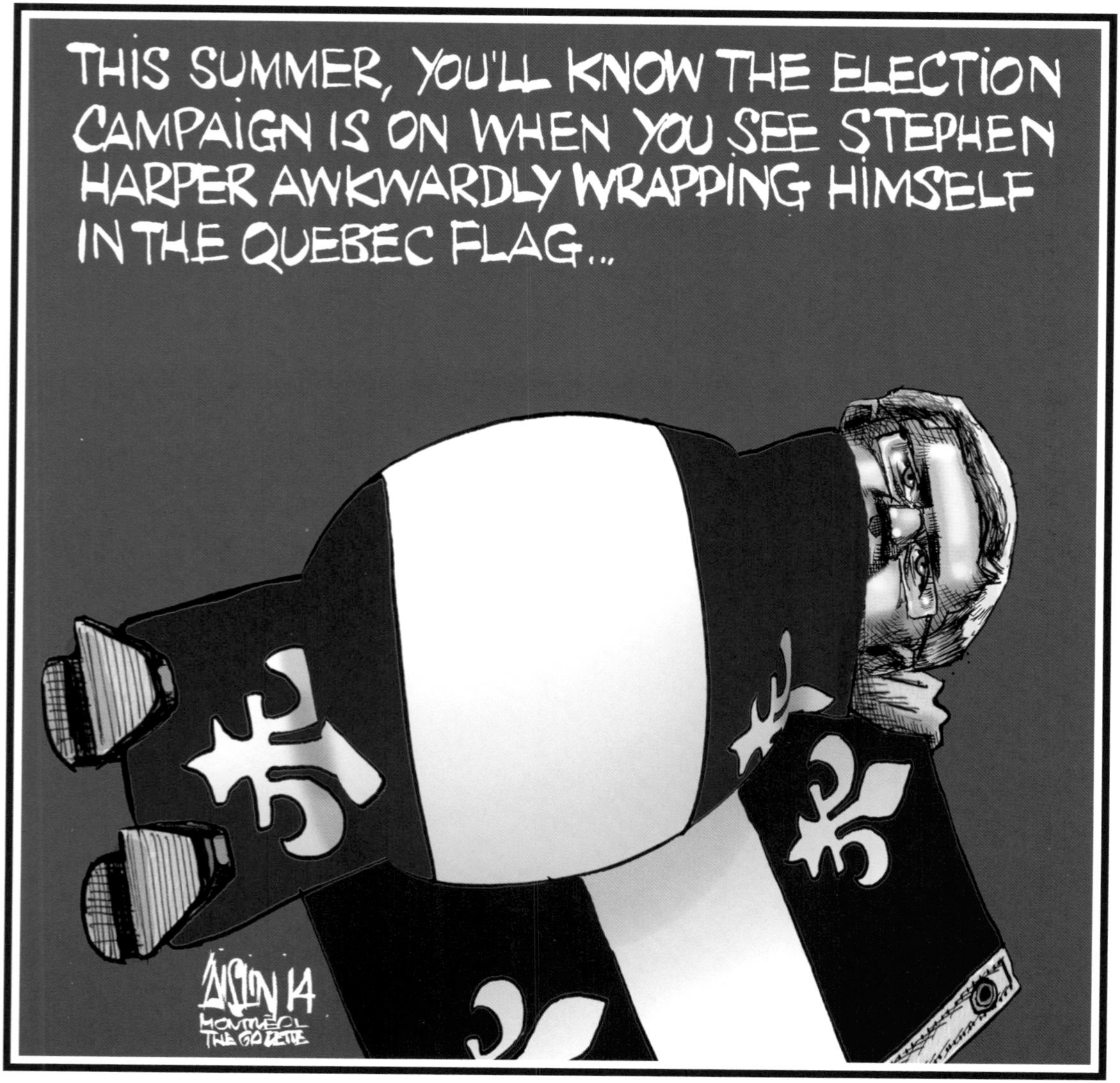
THIS SUMMER, YOU'LL KNOW THE ELECTION CAMPAIGN IS ON WHEN YOU SEE STEPHEN HARPER AWKWARDLY WRAPPING HIMSELF IN THE QUEBEC FLAG...
AISLIN 14
MONTREAL THE GAZETTE

THIS SUMMER, YOU'LL KNOW THE ELECTION CAMPAIGN IS ON WHEN YOU SEE JUSTIN TRUDEAU PHOTOBOMBING HIS WAY FROM COAST to COAST to COAST...

Jim Flaherty proves to be a popular Minister of Finance, producing nine successive sensible, if boring, budgets.

Senator Mike Duffy claims that P.E.I. is the location of his prime residence, despite spending most of his time in Nepean.

Let's rebrand the Senate!

Stephen Harper claims to know nothing about a personal cheque cut to Mike Duffy by his chief of staff, Nigel Wright.

Senator Pamela Wallin returns some of her expense money.

Ottawa's hockey team, the Senators.

RCMP lay 31 criminal charges against Mike Duffy.

Stephen Harper has little to say about the disgraced Senators, most of whom he appointed.

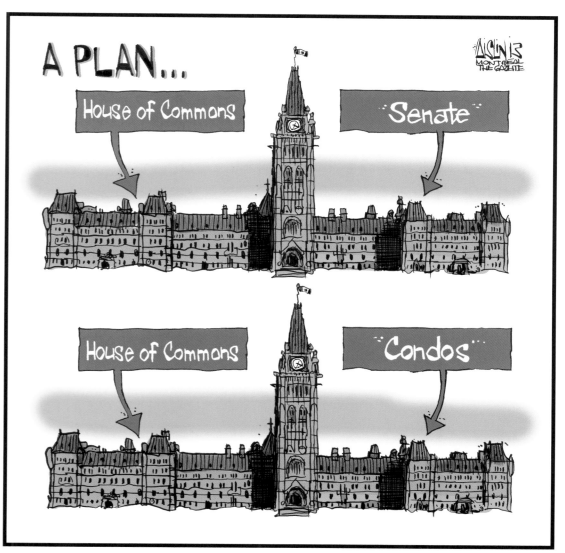

And if we were to abolish the Senate?

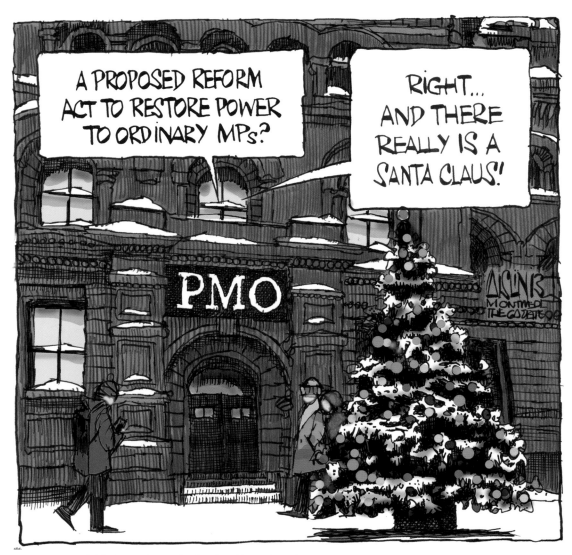

Little chance of this happening under Stephen Harper's regime.

Stephen Harper may be Canada's most autocratic Prime Minister – ever.

No one seems to have the nerve to tell the Prime Minister that he is a terrible singer.

WANTED
Mediocre drummer to back up awful singer.
Apply to 24 Sussex Drive, Ottawa, Ont.

The drummer in PM Stephen Harper's band faces multiple charges of sexual assault and sexual interference.

Replacing Canada's helicopters?

Replacing Canada's jets?

The Conservative Party of Canada is falling into disrepair.

78

Three RCMP officers are shot and killed by a heavily-armed gunman in Moncton.

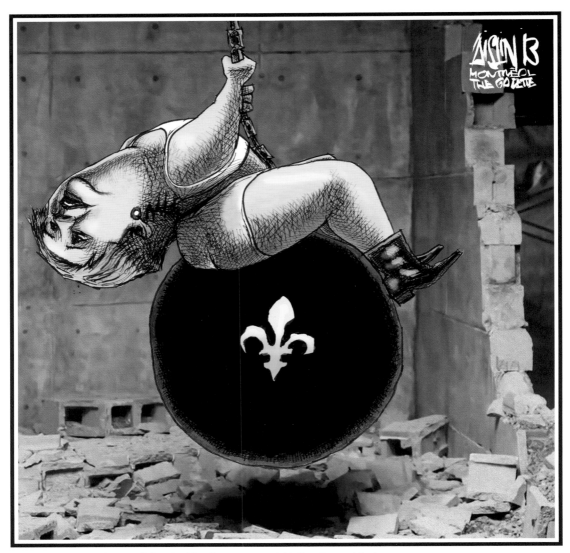

Quebec's own Wrecking Ball, inspired by the controversial Miley Cyrus video!

Quebec

When I first saw the video of Miley Cyrus swinging on a wrecking ball, my immediate thought was to add a few pounds to her so that the image could morph into Quebec's then-Premier Pauline Marois. That's how one of my favourite cartoons of the last two years came to be, summing up the brief reign of the Parti Québécois under Marois from September 2012 to April 2014.

As a minority government, the PQ was desperate for an issue that would rouse the indignation of francophone Québécois in the hope that they would then re-elect the PQ with a majority. The centrepiece of the PQ's election campaign became the Quebec Charter of Values – a charter that would ban the wearing of religious symbols by anyone in the employ of the provincial government. However the campaign failed badly due to mishaps and some questionable tactics employed by the PQ.

The Marois government was defeated with the election of a Liberal majority under new leader Philippe Couillard.

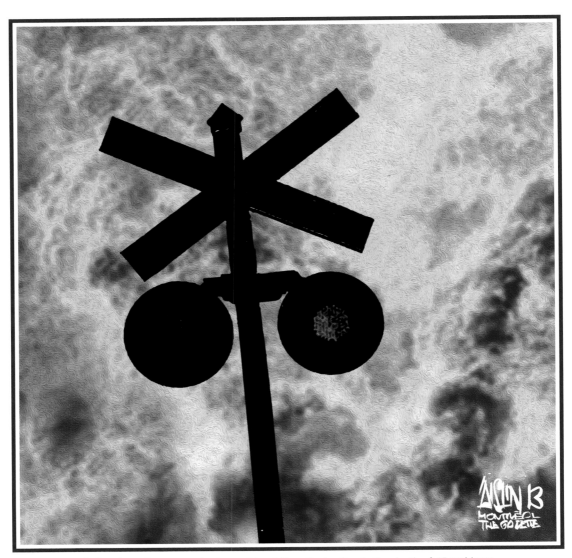

A derailment of oil tankers devastates the town of Lac-Mégantic, leading to the death of 47 residents.

The tragedy in Lac-Mégantic leads to an outpouring of sympathy from all Quebeckers and throughout Canada.

During the Sochi Olympics, both Pauline Marois and Justin Trudeau make unfortunate comments about the event.

84

Celebrating possible tougher language laws at the Office québécois de la langue française.

Employees at a Montreal IGA store are told by management that they are not to speak English amongst themselves.

After the OQLF warns an upscale restaurant against using the word "pasta," I gave Marois a new spaghetti hairdo!

There is a suspicion in Quebec that corruption has always been with us.

A construction boom is underway in Quebec with the new super hospitals.

Police catch mob boss Nicolo Rizzuto on video stuffing cash into his socks.

ITEM: Mob boss received whopping tax refund...

And then...

Tales of corruption at the Charbonneau Commission hearings provide entertainment for Quebeckers.

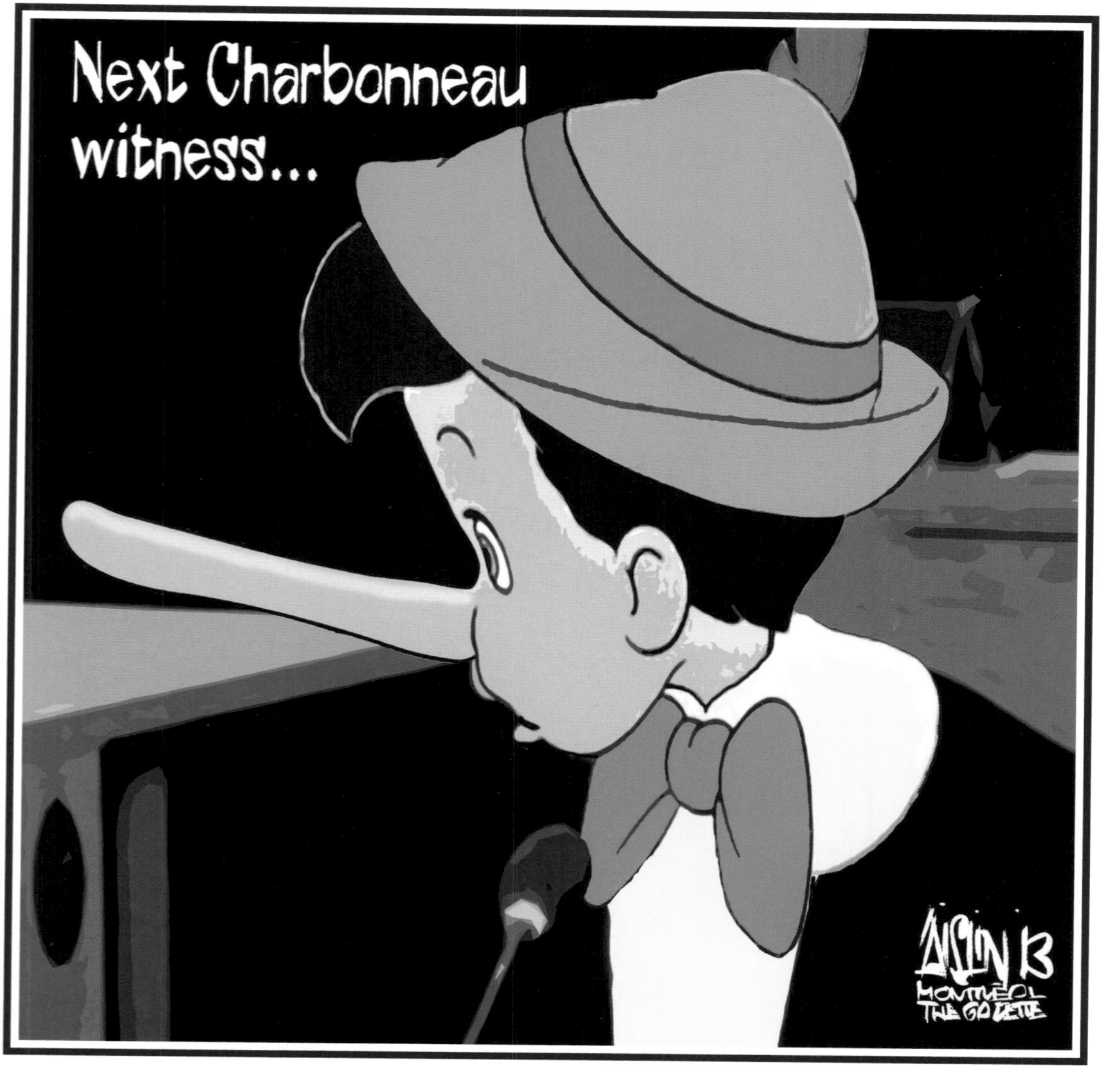
Next Charbonneau
witness...

Parti Québécois minister Jean-François Lisée tries to ingratiate himself with Quebec's Anglophones.

In order to win a majority government, the Parti Québécois know that they will need a rousing cause.

95

VIVE LE QUÉBEC DIVISÉ...

PQ cabinet minister Bernard Drainville is chosen to be the flag-bearer for the proposed Quebec Charter of Values.

The Parti Québécois chooses an election issue that becomes an insult to some Quebeckers.

During hearings for the proposed Charter of Values witnesses present numerous points of view.

98

QUÉBEC

AISLIN 14
MONTRÉAL
THE GAZETTE

The 2014 Quebec election provides a clear choice between separatist Pauline Marois and federalist Philippe Couillard.

Coalition Avenir Québec leader François Legault hopes to position himself between the PQ and the Liberals.

Pauline Marois recruits right-wing businessman Pierre Karl Péladeau as a high-profile candidate.

Separation...

Despite all of the election rhetoric, sovereignty seems less and less of a viable choice for Quebeckers.

The Parti Québécois campaign flounders with the Quebec Values issue and loses the election to the Liberals.

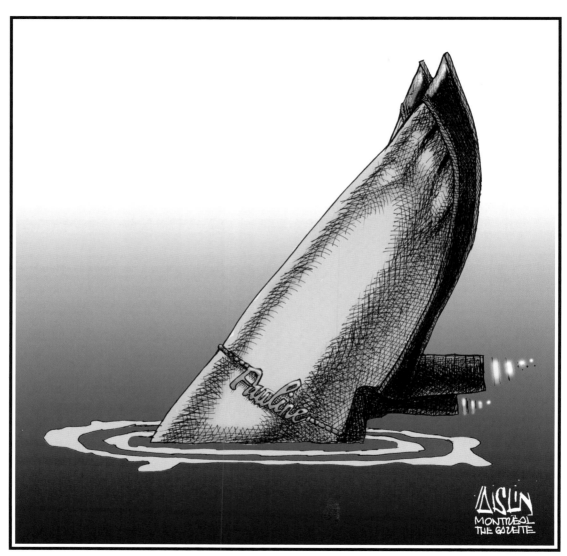

Pauline Marois is sunk. ˉ

Bernard Drainville meets his Waterloo.

Newly-elected Bloc Québécois leader Mario Beaulieu shoots himself in the foot with his acceptance speech.

New Quebec Premier Philippe Couillard will now try to repair the damage and lead Quebec into the future.

A slice of Montreal's multicultural life.

Montreal

Montreal is an acquired taste. Visitors will often ask how I can still put up with my home town after all these years – with our crumbling infrastructure, endless traffic tie-ups, the highest taxes in North America, corruption on all sides, never-ending language squabbles, loud and strident street demonstrations, the arrogance of municipal workers, and so on, and so on.

The answer is an easy one: I'm a cartoonist! I also love this place. Indeed for me it's the most interesting city in Canada, as it is for many Montrealers who have gone on to careers elsewhere. Some come back from time to time, such as the actor Jay Baruchel (above), who returned to host the 2013 Just for Laughs festival.

Dr. Arthur Porter made many friends during his time in Montreal as the Director General and CEO of the MUHC...

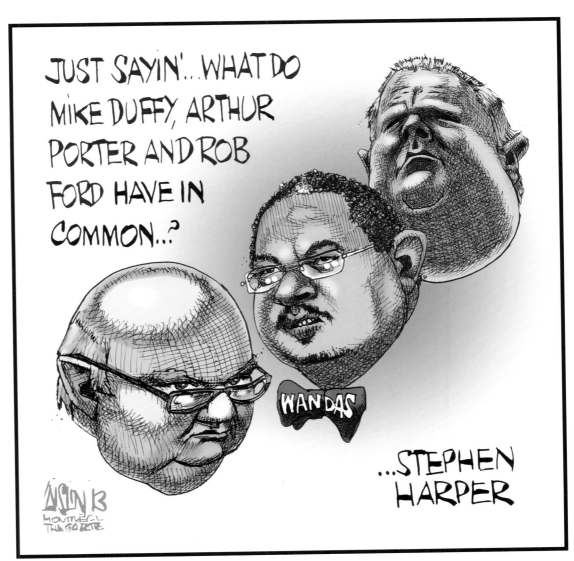

...and even more good friends throughout Canada.

Questionable business dealings by Porter lead to his rapid resignation and move to the Bahamas.

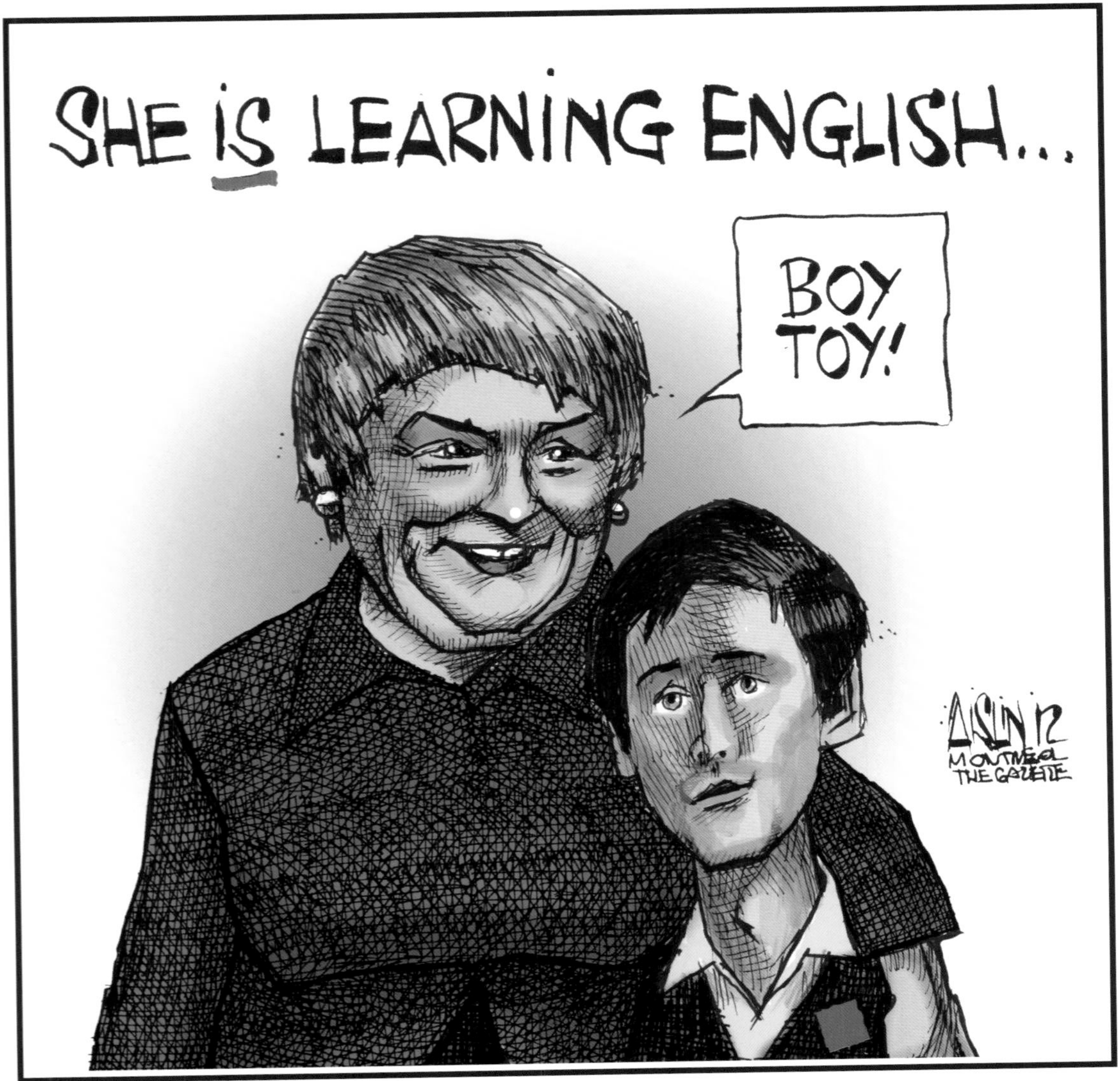
SHE IS LEARNING ENGLISH...
BOY TOY!
AISLIN 12
MONTREAL THE GAZETTE

Marois and the PQ endorse the striking red-square students and their leaders, including cute Léo Bureau-Blouin.

AND NOW, TATTOOS...

The student protests go on for months with the red squares becoming the ubiquitous symbol against tuition hikes.

The police are always on duty during the protest rallies against tuition increases.

Merchants and service people will greet customers in Montreal with a "Bonjour! Hi!..."

...unless, of course, the customer is a Parti Québécois militant.

No one seems surprised when chunks of cement fall from a Highway 40 overpass into Montreal traffic.

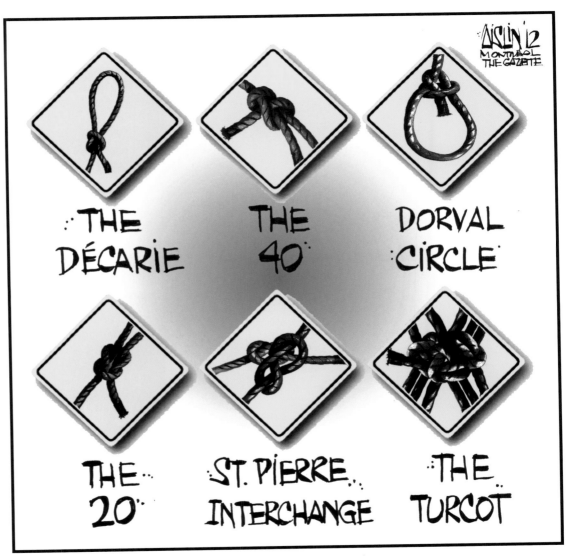

Here are some suggestions for caution signs at key Montreal traffic interchanges.

Motorist vs. cyclist – a never-ending conflict.

Despite the condition of its roads, Montreal remains one of the best cycling cities in the world.

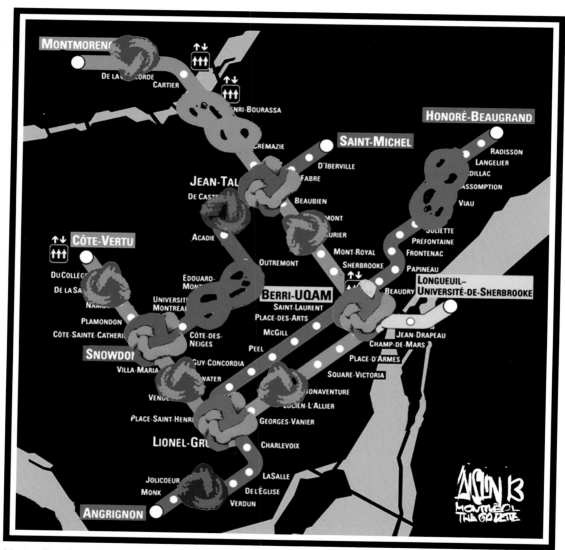

Montreal's aging subway system is constantly breaking down.

The cheapest solution to Montreal's transportation problems?

Montreal comes up with some temporary solutions until the crumbling Champlain Bridge can be replaced.

In the wake of damning testimony at the Charbonneau Commission.

Claiming innocence, Montreal mayor Gérald Tremblay resigns after allegations made at the Charbonneau Commission.

The interim mayor, former city councillor Michael Applebaum, resigns after being indicted on a number of charges.

For a period of time, Montreal is rudderless.

WHO SHOULD BE MONTREAL'S NEXT MAYOR? HERE ARE 3 POSSIBILITIES...

Send your picks to: aislin@montrealgazette.com

GÉRARD D. LAFLAQUE

THE COMEDY FESTIVAL MASCOT

THE ST. HUBERT B.B.Q. CHICKEN

AISLIN '13
MONTREAL
THE GAZETTE

The Gazette runs a tongue-in-cheek online contest asking readers to choose a new mayor.

The Saint-Hubert BBQ chicken – fast, efficient, cost-effective, and bilingual – wins in a landslide.

In the municipal election of 2013, who would desperate Montrealers be voting for?

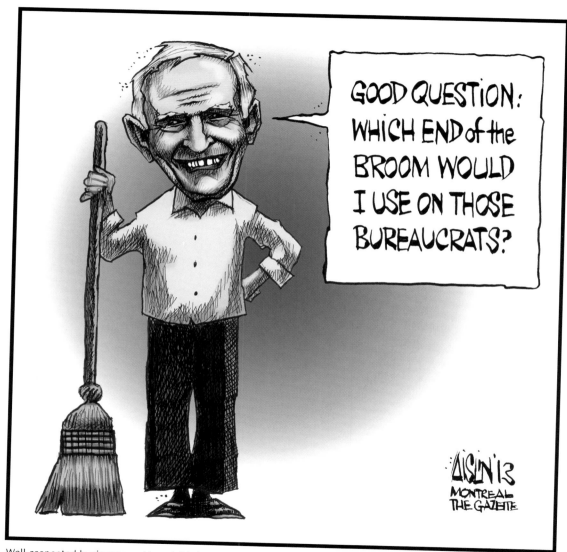

Well-respected businessman Marcel Côté runs for mayor, promising to clean up City Hall.

Veteran Projet Montréal leader Richard Bergeron calls for a new tram system to solve the city's transportation woes.

A new young candidate, Mélanie Joli, keeps rising in the polls – but not quickly enough to catch up to...

...the eventual winner, mayoral candidate Denis Coderre, who doesn't even bother putting up election posters.

Immediately after his election, new Montreal mayor Denis Coderre tweets some managerial advice to the Habs.

Sports

Psychologists may tell you that we all need an enemy. It's a hard-wired survival mechanism from our caveman days, there to protect us from the dangers of the unknown. Leaders have taken advantage of this throughout history in order to justify leading us into war, sometimes unnecessarily, with the premise that "we" are good and "they" are evil.

The same principle applies to our love of sports – and I'm all for it! I far prefer hating the Boston Bruins to hating another country. Sport is a lot more fun to watch on TV, too, particularly now that I have a 48-inch HD television set. The detail is great – showing every emotion on a player's face!

I'll hazard a guess that I draw more sports-related cartoons than most other North American editorial cartoonists. The Gazette appreciates this, knowing that even though Montreal is such a multi-cultural city, we are united around sports, particularly with our Habs.

In 2013, the once-mighty Montreal Alouettes place 3rd, with record losses in the Eastern Division of the CFL.

The Grey Cup is always the last big outdoor sporting event that Canadians enjoy before hibernating for the winter.

Milos Raonic's terrific performances in international tennis matches increase Canadians' interest in the game...

...and doubly so when Westmount's Eugénie Bouchard reaches the finals at Wimbledon.

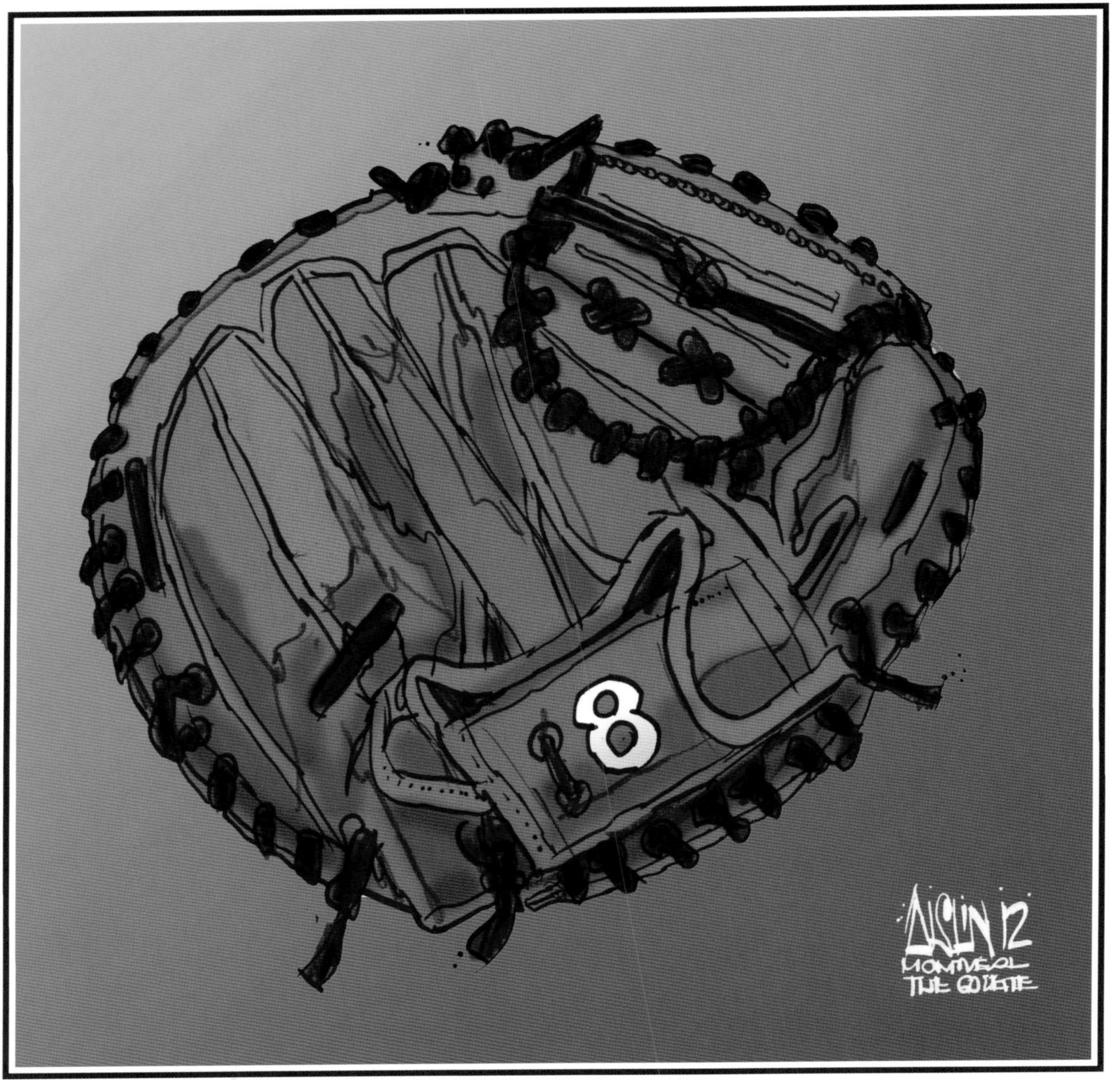
8
AISLIN 12
MONTREAL
THE GAZETTE

Gary Carter: 1954 – 2012.

International outrage over Russia's anti-gay laws leading up to the Sochi Olympic Games.

We see great performances from Canadian Olympic athletes in Sochi, but not from certain politicians back home.

Marie-Philip Poulin's achievements at the Sochi Olympics easily compare to Paul Henderson's in Moscow in 1972.

After the Olympics finish, Canadian hockey fans have to get back to the shenanigans taking place in the NHL.

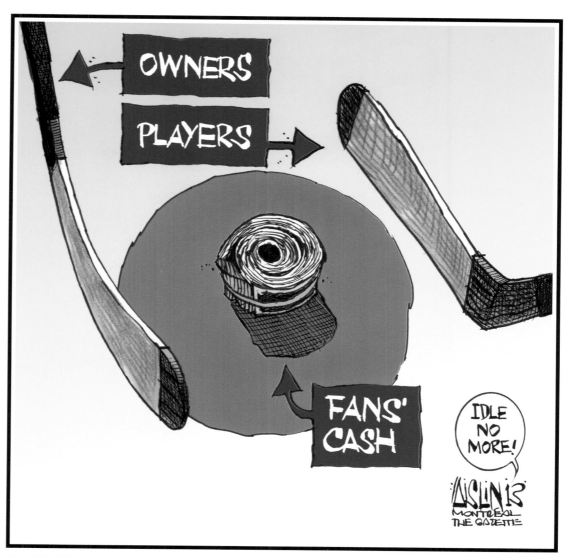

The 2012-2013 NHL lockout – over money – is finally settled.

Canadian television personality George Stroumboulopoulos is named the new anchor of Hockey Night in Canada.

Veteran broadcaster Don Cherry will no doubt be watching with great interest.

The Habs finally defeat the Boston Bruins in the 2014 playoffs...

...much of that due to the amazing performance of Habs defenceman P. K. Subban.

No Canadian-based NHL team has won the Stanley Cup since 1993.

Nevertheless, Habs fans have very high hopes for the future.

The 2014 World Cup kicks off in Brazil.

However, Brazil is eliminated by Germany in the semi-finals with the embarrassing score of 7 to 1.

The World Cup final begins.

1972 Russia-Canada Hockey Series

by Terry Mosher (Aislin)

To celebrate the 40th anniversary of the Canada-Russia Summit Series, *Canada's History Magazine* asked me to write a memoir of my visit to Moscow to cover the event away back in 1972. It was also decided that I would colourize the original sketches that I had drawn for my newspaper, *The Montreal Gazette*. In 2012, the article – reprinted here – won the 2012 gold National Magazine Award in the Words and Pictures category.

Goal #1

Goal #2

Goal #3

Goal #4

Drowning our sorrows

Forty years ago, Toe Blake's Tavern was a busy place on any Saturday night. But on the night of September 2nd, 1972, the place was jammed to its fluorescent-lit rafters with patrons wanting to watch the first game of the momentous Canada-Russia hockey series. The game was being played a few short blocks away in the old Montreal Forum. We arrived early to ensure we had seats. I was with my pal Nick Auf der Maur, a notorious local journalist, boulevardier and left-leaning gadfly. He was the only person in the room cheering for the Soviets. The mood in the room was like that all over Canada – initial optimistic euphoria that rapidly changed to shock and anger as the Soviet team quickly gained the upper hand. I sketched the souring faces around me after each successive Russian goal, ending with a final doodle of a beaming Auf der Maur after Russian goal numbers seven!

After the drawings ran in my newspaper, *The Montreal Gazette*, I was asked to illustrate a book on the series that would be written by Jack Ludwig. A three-way deal between *The Montreal Gazette*, McClelland & Stewart and *Maclean's* magazine was arranged to pay my way to Moscow. What follows are my notes and cartoons following each successive game.

Goal #5

Goal #6

Goal #7

What's in a name?

The second game was played in Toronto. I again watched alongside a nervous crowd in Toe Blake's. Cautious relief was expressed after Canada won the game handily 4–1. Several of our players put up sterling performances, including Montreal hometown favourites Yvan Cournoyer and Serge Savard.

In the tavern, we noted that the legendary Toronto hockey broadcaster, Foster Hewitt, had done his homework by thoroughly memorizing the names of all of the Soviet players. However, as usual, and typical of many English-speaking Canadians, Hewitt mangled the pronunciation of all of the French-Canadian players' names.

Party on, comrades

Being the last minute, the only way my backers could get me on a flight to Russia was by squeezing me onto a pre-organized Canada-Russia hockey tour along with my boyhood idol, Maurice Richard. For a young cartoonist, this was a dream assignment.

On the airplane, everyone was given a free bottle of Canadian whiskey and a carton of cigarettes. So, I remember little of the journey. Furthermore, in Moscow, the discomfort of dealing with incessant lineups, confusing hotel arrangements, language difficulties, and KGB guys in pointed shoes (really) was rounded off at the corners by my discovery of cheap red-pepper vodka in the Berezka tourist stores.

The worst that happened to us – the only time Rocket Richard blew his gasket – was at the end of our stay, when bus officials would not let our group leave for the airport for two hours until someone returned a room key that had been stolen as a souvenir. Anyway, we were there for the hockey. And what great hockey it was!

Child's play

What had become apparent to observant Canadians during the 1972 series was that Russian coaching techniques had advanced well beyond those being used in Canada. As Team Canada coach Harry Sinden put it, "I haven't seen any Russian that couldn't play in the NHL." Well thought-out exercises and techniques were being applied in a thorough and academic way to talented youngsters, even at a very early age.

Authorities told Jack Ludwig that the Soviet hockey program forbids bodychecks for the first seven or eight years of play in the little leagues. Instead, emphasis was placed on skating, durability skills and muscle development.

Getting schooled

The action for Game 3 shifted to Winnipeg, where one of the hardest-fought games of the whole series ended in a 4–4 tie. I realized, watching this game, that Soviet winger Valeri Kharlamov was one of the best hockey players I had ever seen. He dazzled us with crisp discipline that we had not witnessed in our NHL stars for some time.

Later, as the action shifted to Moscow, four players, including New York Ranger forward Vic Hadfield, decided to go home because they were getting little or no ice time. Hadfield had failed to score in the two games he had played in Canada, and was told he would sit out the rest of the series in Moscow. Critics attacked Hadfield and the other players, saying they had chickened out.

the KHARLAMOV
Summer Hockey School

skate like a HOWIE MORENZ

stickhandle like a MAX BENTLEY

shoot like a CHARLIE CONACHER

score goals like a ROCKET RICHARD

the VIC HADFIELD
Summer Hockey School

swear like a PHIL ESPOSITO

hustle like a ROD GILBERT

dress like a MICKEY REDMOND

skate like an ALAN EAGLESON

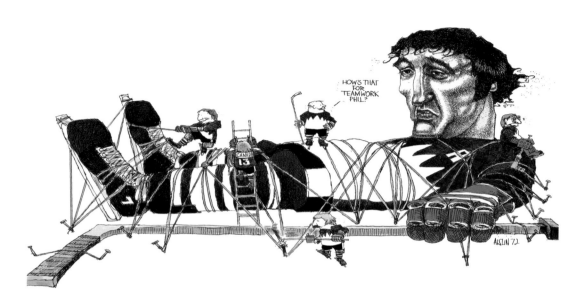

HOW'S THAT FOR TEAMWORK PHIL?

Fit to be tied

With Game 4 in Vancouver, Team Canada hit bottom. In fact, the final score of 5–3 in favour of the Soviets didn't really reflect how badly the Canadians played. Brad Park, Frank Mahovlich, Vic Hadfield, and Rod Gilbert played like rank amateurs. Furthermore, the great Ken Dryden had let in twelve goals in the two games that he had played in Montreal and Vancouver!

The only Canadian player who continued to carry the flag high in Vancouver was the relentless Phil Esposito. After the game, I drew Esposito as a frustrated Gulliver being tied to the ground by his incompetent Lilliputian teammates. When Esposito later saw the cartoon, he told me that if it was printed he personally would wipe the floor with my (then) very long hair. Presumably Esposito did not realize the cartoon of him was a favourable one.

However, things were about to turn around for Team Canada. And I am convinced that the fans' enthusiasm, both in the arena and encouragement received from home, pumped up the adrenalin in the Team Canada players.

♪ O YAKUSHEV,
WHY MUST WE BE SO BLAND?
TRITE AND CONTENT,
WITH CAMPBELL AND HIS BAND!

ON HOCKEY NIGHT,
WE'LL ALL GET TIGHT,
AND WATCH THE C.B.C.

SEE ROUSTABOUTS,
'TWEEN K.C. SCOUTS,
AND WASHINGTON, D.C!

O YAKUSHEV,
DESPITE YOUR REFEREE,
O YAKUSHEV, PLEASE LISTEN TO MY PLEA!

O YAKUSHEV,
WON'T YOU DEFECT FOR ME?!!

Woe, Canada!

Game 5 – the first game in Moscow – started out well enough for Team Canada, with the team leading by 3–0 at the beginning of the third period. But then, inspired by the fast play of Aleksandr Yakushev, Russian players scored five times in the third period. Final score: Russia 5, Canada 4. Some Canadians then expressed a wish that, instead of Hadfield returning home, Yakushev had defected to Canada!

Game faces

When I took on this assignment, I was handed a bag full of expensive camera equipment and press photographer credentials. My newspaper was going to let the Russians know that I was a political cartoonist! Therefore, I was positioned at ice level in the photographers' section of the Luzhniki Ice Palace in Moscow. Often, I would look up into the crowd for possible character sketches.

There were so many *militsia* – military types – in the arena that, at first, I thought they were ushers. All three thousand Canadian fans looked like a typical group that had come to celebrate a Grey Cup weekend, complete with horns, cowbells, placards, and thousands of Canadian flags in every conceivable size and shape. In contrast, the Russian fans were all dressed in bland blues, greys and blacks. By the final game, however, the Russians had learned to be just as loud as the boisterous Canucks – they incessantly whistled their displeasure.

What the Hull?!?

Winnipegers were angered by the fact that Team Canada had excluded any members of the renegade World Hockey Association league from playing in the series, including hometown star Bobby Hull of the Winnipeg Jets. Therefore, I drew a popular cartoon suggesting Prime Minister Pierre Trudeau and federal Amateur Sports Minister John Munro launch Hull into the action, where he deserved to be if this was supposedly a team of Canada's best players.

Mugged

Here is an interesting footnote: A number of years later, I was giving a speech in Montreal about the art of political cartooning. I hadn't noticed that former NHL president Clarence Campbell was in the audience. He approached me after the talk and congratulated me, saying that he thoroughly enjoyed my work.

However, he added, some cartoonist had drawn an awful cartoon of him during the Canada-Russia hockey series of 1972, taking the Stanley Cup into a pawn shop. He wondered if I had ever seen the cartoon and who that terrible cartoonist was?

"Sorry, Mr. Campbell," I replied, "I have no idea who might have drawn that cartoon!"

On the Summit

In what seemed like a gigantic whirl of Canadian flags and uniforms, Canada would win the final three games to win the series, even if Russia scored more goals overall. Great final performances from Phil Esposito, Yvan Cournoyer, Bobby Clarke and others would save the day, along with the great comeback performance of Ken Dryden in Game 8 when it counted most.

But the most miraculous feat during the whole series had to be that of Paul Henderson, a journeyman NHL player who rose to the occasion by scoring seven goals in this series, including the winner in the final three games.

Most Canadians of a certain age – say, over forty-five – remember exactly what they were doing when Paul Henderson scored his famous goal on September 28, 1972. But, despite being at ice level, I missed seeing the goal. Skeptic that I am, I was convinced that the Soviets would score a final winning goal, so I was at the other end of the rink.

The Wrecking Ball is Aislin's forty-seventh book.
More information is available at: **www.aislin.com**

Other books with Aislin cartoons:

Aislin–100 Caricatures (1971)
Hockey Night in Moscow (1972, with Jack Ludwig)
Aislin–150 Caricatures (1973)
The Great Hockey Thaw (1974, with Jack Ludwig)
'Ello, Morgentaler? Aislin–150 Caricatures (1975)
O.K. Everybody Take a Valium! Aislin–150 Caricatures (1977)
L'Humour d'Aislin (1977)
The Retarded Giant (1977, with Bill Mann)
The Hecklers: A History of Canadian Political Cartooning
   (1979, with Peter Desbarats)
The Year The Expos Almost Won the Pennant
   (1979, with Brodie Snyder)
Did the Earth Move? Aislin–180 Caricatures (1980)
The Year The Expos Finally Won Something
   (1981, with Brodie Snyder)
The First Great Canadian Trivia Quiz
   (1981, with Brodie Snyder)
Stretchmarks (1982)
The Anglo Guide to Survival in Quebec
   (1983, with various Montreal writers)

Tootle: A Children's Story (1984, with Johan Sarrazin)
Where's the Trough? (1985)
Old Whores (1987)
Aislin: 20 Years (1987)
What's the Big Deal? (1988, with Rick Salutin)
The Lawn Jockey (1989)
Parcel of Rogues (1990, with Maude Barlow)
Barbed Lyres, Canadian Venomous Verse
   (1990, with Margaret Atwood and other Canadian poets)
Drawing Bones–15 Years of Cartooning Brian Mulroney (1991)
Put Up & Shut Up! The 90s so far in Cartoons
   (1994, with Hubie Bauch)
Oh, Canadians! Hysterically Historical Rhymes
   (1996, with Gordon Snell)
One Oar in the Water: The Nasty 90s continued in cartoons (1997)
Oh, No! More Canadians! Hysterically Historical Rhymes
   (1998, with Gordon Snell)
Nick : A Montreal Life (1998, with Dave Bist, L. Ian Macdonald,
   Stephen Phizicky)
2000 Reasons to Hate the Millennium
   (1999, with Josh Freed and other contributors)
The Big Wind-Up! The final book of Nasty 90s cartoons (1999)
Yes! Even More Canadians! Hysterically Historical Rhymes
   (2000, with Gordon Snell)
The Oh, Canadians Omnibus (2001, with Gordon Snell)
In Your Face ... other recent cartoons (2001)
More Marvellous Canadians! (2002, with Gordon Snell)
The Illustrated Canadian Songbook, (2003, with Bowser & Blue)
Further Fabulous Canadians! (2004, with Gordon Snell)
OH,OH! ...and other recent cartoons (2004)
The Best Of OH! CANADIANS (2006, with Gordon Snell)
Mordecai Richler Was Here (2006, with Mordecai Richler)
What Next? ...and other recent cartoons by Aislin (2006)
Aislin's Shenanigans ...and other recent cartoons by Aislin (2009)
Finn's Thin Book of Irish Ironies (2010, with Patrick Watson)
Caricature • Cartoon Canada, edited by Terry Mosher (2012)
Was It Good For You?...and other recent cartoons by Aislin (2012)
Up, Up, & Away – the Montreal Expos (2014, with Jonah Keri))

More information and additional cartoons are available on
Facebook, on Twitter and at www.aislin.com

Montreal's McCord Museum has an online database of over 5,000
Aislin cartoons: http://www.musee-mccord.qc.ca